D0772370

BARRY HANNAH
Postmodern Romantic

RUTH D. WESTON

Louisiana State University Press *Baton Rouge*

Designer: Michele Myatt Quinn
Typeface: Adobe Garamond
Typesetter: Wilsted & Taylor Publishing Services
Printer and binder: Thomson-Shore, Inc.

Part of Chapter 1 was first published as " 'The Whole Lying Opera of It': Dreams, Lies, and Confessions in the Fiction of Barry Hannah," *Mississippi Quarterly*, XLIV (Summer, 1991), 411–28, and is reprinted by permission. Portions of Chapter 2 were first published as "Debunking the Unitary Self and Story in the War Stories of Barry Hannah," *Southern Literary Journal*, XXVII (Spring, 1995), 96–106, and are reprinted by permission. Part of Chapter 3 first appeared as "Debunking Some Illusions About Self and Story in the Surfiction of Barry Hannah," in *Creative and Critical Approaches to the Short Story*, ed. Noel Harold Kaylor, Jr. (Lewiston, N.Y.: Edwin Mellen Press, 1997), 289–303, and is reprinted by permission of Noel Harold Kaylor, Jr., and Mellen Press. Portions of Chapter 2 and 4 were also published as "Review of Barry Hannah's *High Lonesome*" in *Short Story*, V (Fall, 1997), 107–12, and are reprinted by permission.

Library of Congress Cataloging-in-Publication Data
Weston, Ruth D., 1934–
    Barry Hannah, postmodern romantic / Ruth D. Weston
      p.   cm. — (Southern literary studies ; vol.)
    Includes bibliographical references and index.
    ISBN 0-8071-2290-4 (cloth : alk. paper)
    1. Hannah, Barry—Criticism and interpretation.   2. Romanticism—
Southern States—History—20th century.   3. Postmodernism
(Literature)—Southern States.   4. Mississippi—In literature.
I. Series.
PS3558.A476Z94   1998
813'.54—dc21
                                      98-24407
                                        CIP

BARRY HANNAH

Postmodern Romantic

Southern Literary Studies
Fred Hobson, Editor

for

Lauren, Taylor, and Sarah

Contents

Acknowledgments • xi

Abbreviations • xiii

Introduction: The Reticent Beauty of Barry Hannah's Fiction • 1

O N E
Romance and Rage in the American Man-Child • 10

T w o
Battles for Identity: Debunking the Unitary Self and Story • 41

T H R E E
Storytellers and Other Interesting Monsters: From Oral History
to Postmodern Narrative • 73

F o u r
Hannah's Comic Vision: Riffs on Language, Literature,
and the "Play" of Life • 104

Bibliography • 133

Index • 141

Acknowledgments

When Bob Brinkmeyer asked me, in 1989, to consider writing about Barry Hannah's fiction, I was not sure that I could. I had then read very little of Hannah; but my department chair, Bill Epperson, who has always read everything, quickly lent me his copies of Hannah's books. I thank them both. I am grateful for the support of the administration of Oral Roberts University and for the cheerful assistance of Carolyn Baker, Thelma Burden, and the ORU interlibrary loan staff; and for my English department "family," including secretary Wanda Fisher.

I am indebted to Robert Bly for a book that was to be one of my first keys to understanding Hannah's fiction, and to poet Ken McCullough, who, at a writer's workshop in Tulsa in 1990, told me that *Iron John* was to come out soon. I also thank Marcia Jacobson for her *Being a Boy Again: Autobiography and the American Boy Book,* another significant source that was published just when I needed it. Similarly, for keys to Hannah, to the short story, and to literature in general and the teaching of it, I am continually thankful for Mary Rohrberger, not only for her own scholarship but also for that of the scholars she has always gathered around her, whether at the South Central Modern Language Association, when her academic home was Oklahoma State University; or in the pages of *Short Story,* the journal she founded; or at meetings of the International Conference on the Short Story in English, which she began and still sponsors in her "retirement" from the University of Northern Iowa. As will be clear in this book, the ideas of some of those scholars have helped me to express my own ideas about Barry Hannah's fiction.

I am also grateful for the support of the English department at the United States Military Academy, West Point, when I was a visiting professor there (1993–94) during the early drafting of this manuscript, and especially for the administrative and collegial support of Colonel Peter Stromberg, English department head, and Colonel John Calabro, my military sponsor. This book is the better for my conversations about literature and life with many of my West Point colleagues, especially Colonel Joseph Cox and Captain John Hannah (no relation to Barry), and others of the West Point–Chapel Hill connection. I am especially grateful to Joe Cox for pointing out important reading materials on Vietnam and for sharing some of his Vietnam experiences through his poems. For their encouragement and support of my Hannah research in various ways, I thank Bob Phillips at the *Mississippi Quarterly;* Fred Hobson, who asked me to do the book; and John Easterly and Catherine Kadair at Louisiana State University Press. Wendy Jacobs edited the manuscript with professionalism.

For their "deeply" strange, as Hannah might say, and honest comments on Hannah's stories, I thank my students and visiting faculty colleagues in the senior seminar "Voices of the Modern South": John Affleck, Jenni Enns, Linda Gray, Tommy Hale, Sunshine America (Sunny) Kruse-Shafer, Neal Locke, Kate Meyers, and Jennifer Naylor. Kate, who is not only scholar-editor-friend but also close at hand, kindly read the entire manuscript. Special thanks go to Jean Germany Mosley, a high school classmate of Barry Hannah's and now a professor of education at Oral Roberts University, who told the class about some of the experiences shared between her family and the Hannah family in Clinton, Mississippi; and to Jean's husband, who tells me that Barry was his idol as a high school trumpet player. Jean and Mike could hardly wait to read the manuscript.

For his continuing mentorship and friendship over some twenty-five years, I am grateful to Winston Weathers, professor emeritus at the University of Tulsa. For the inestimable comfort of in-house computer expertise and other support of matters literary, I thank my husband, Kenneth C. Weston, also professor emeritus, the University of Tulsa. Finally, I wish to thank Barry Hannah, not only for his wild, wise, and brave stories but also for his gracious responses to my queries. Any error of fact or misreading of his fiction is, of course, my own.

ABBREVIATIONS

A   *Airships*

B   *Boomerang*

BOH   *Bats Out of Hell*

CM   *Captain Maximus*

GR   *Geronimo Rex*

HJ   *Hey Jack!*

HL   *High Lonesome*

N   *Nightwatchmen*

ND   *Never Die*

R   *Ray*

TH   *The Tennis Handsome*

BARRY HANNAH
Postmodern Romantic

Introduction:
The Reticent Beauty of Barry Hannah's Fiction

We have observed that the finest story writers seem to be in one
sense obstructionists.
—Eudora Welty, *The Eye of the Story*

WHEN I BEGAN my research on Hannah, I had been strangely fascinated
by his fiction for several years, puzzling over his complex stories; marveling
at his mastery at storytelling and his virtuosity with language; and yet, as a
woman and a feminist, horrified by his depiction of, and his characters'
treatment of, women. My reaction was at least as strong as that of David
Madden, who, after reading *Geronimo Rex,* said, "I simultaneously loved
the effect of and despised the sensibility behind each line." Hannah's is not
a "politically correct" fiction; but what deserving of the name of literature
is? Robert H. Brinkmeyer, Jr., calls him one of the "bad boys" of contemporary southern fiction, among whom Brinkmeyer also includes Harry
Crews (in *A Feast of Snakes*) and Cormac McCarthy (in *Child of God*). By
"bad boys," he means writers who "flaunt . . . southern tradition . . . [or]
turn [it] upside down."[1]

1. David Madden, "Barry Hannah's *Geronimo Rex* in Retrospect," *Southern Review,* XIX
(1983), 315; Robert H. Brinkmeyer, Jr., "Beyond the Veranda: Trends in Contemporary
Southern Literature," paper presented at Oklahoma Foundation for the Humanities symposium "Southern Fried Culture: A New Recipe, A New South, A New Conversation," Tulsa,
Okla., March 1, 1996.

Barry Hannah's fiction bountifully repays the effort required of the reader—and it does require some effort—not only because of its postmodern style but also because of the hard truths Hannah shows us about the conditions of contemporary life. But attentive readers will rejoice in the feast of language, the fun of the irreverence, and the essentially optimistic spirit of Hannah's fiction: the hope against hope, the faith in the midst of doubt, about life, love, literature, and language, with which these stories are presented. Another question of faith is important in Hannah's fiction also: that of faith in and doubt about God, and about the human ability to have religious faith. It is a constant undercurrent in his work, as perhaps should not be surprising in a writer brought up in a Christian home and in a region still known by Flannery O'Connor's description: the "Christ-haunted" South. The stories, the language, and the cadences of the King James Bible, modified by the consumer-oriented rhetoric of present-day telempvangelists, are second nature to Hannah. They are in the very air of the South he lives in and writes about, providing him with a powerful fund of images. One of the most compelling aspects of his fiction is his true ear for the southern vernacular in general and for the language of evangelical Protestantism in particular. Anyone who "talks the talk and walks the walk" of a Southern Baptist, Methodist, Presbyterian, or any number of evangelical or charismatic sects can attest to the veracity of the speech rhythms in this fiction.

Geronimo Rex and *Nightwatchmen,* Hannah's first two novels, are the only ones to exhibit both the novelistic style and the theme of initiation that are the province of the traditional *bildungsroman;* this theme, however, pervades his fiction. Even his stories about adult characters are of a piece with, and cannot be fully appreciated apart from, his stories of adolescent initiation. Especially *Geronimo Rex, Boomerang, Hey Jack!,* and many stories from each of his collections demonstrate Hannah's relation to the tradition of autobiographical writing in general and to the turn-of-the-century "boy book" in particular. Subthemes important to the stories of initiation but that also have relevance to his oeuvre as a whole are those of rage and violence, which result largely from a character's insecurity, from the search for absolutes, and from an unfocused existential malaise not unlike that depicted in the novels of Walker Percy. In Hannah, however, the results of these dysfunctions are often depicted in a mode that parodies the Southern

Gothic. Hannah's treatment of these topics has oblique connections to the fiction of O'Connor and to the American and European confessional novel; his relation to the fiction of both William Faulkner and Ernest Hemingway is much more complex and involves both style and content. A major trope throughout Hannah's fiction is that of the lie, through which Hannah addresses social, cultural, and religious betrayals of the American dream—especially in terms of defective myths about male prowess in sports, in war, and in relationships with women—that affect psychological maturation.

Hannah's boy books for the 1980s and 1990s are essentially nostalgic depictions of the bittersweet childhood of the American male, through autobiographical fictions that reveal clues to important meanings for their adult narrators. In fact, the search for the self is an important theme that develops as Hannah's literary career progresses. And since his fiction is tied not only to his region, the American South, but also to his generation, often called the Vietnam generation, his war stories establish effective metaphors for the battles Hannah's protagonists engage in to establish, perhaps create, coherent identities.

Because of Vietnam, many Americans of all regions who came of age in the late 1960s and early 1970s, both veterans and others, seem to experience an additional level of insecurity about identity beyond the familiar Oedipal complexes. For those southerners who carry the additional burden of a keen sense of cultural history, as Hannah surely does, both the fact of the South's defeat in the Civil War and the traditional versus evolving cultural expectations based on codes of class, race, and gender often complicate the search for a secure sense of self; the resulting complications are reflected in his fiction. Hannah's generation, after all, grew up with Vietnam as well as with the civil rights and feminist movements. Almost all of his stories, especially from *Airships* forward, are informed by war. Indeed, his characters seem haunted by war, especially the Civil War and Vietnam, which often merge in their minds. In *Bats Out of Hell,* an extremely varied collection, Hannah is still concerned with adolescent initiation. The perspective is primarily that of middle-aged men, many of whom have had war experiences, but the settings and subtexts include the Persian Gulf conflict of the early 1990s, known as Desert Storm. Hannah's war stories are also related to other war literature—especially the literature about Vietnam—by both combatants and noncombatants; and his continuing development of a more postmodern style is comparable to that of other writers who create war literature. The search for self is also seen in stories that reflect the American cult of youth—the battle against old age and the accompanying loss of virility. Hannah treats this phenomenon throughout his work, significantly in "Get Some Young," one of his finest stories, which is from his latest collection, *High Lonesome.*

A particular aspect of identity of interest to Hannah is that of the special problems of extraordinary achievers: people Hannah calls "interesting monsters." These include war heroes, sports figures, musicians, writers, and other storytellers, such as Hannah himself. To the extent that these figures are larger than life and usually obsessed with one facet of their experience of truth, they are less than fully rounded human beings, and thus they are avatars of what Sherwood Anderson called "grotesques": characters whose visions, and thus lives, are distorted. Primary among these figures are Hannah's many liar characters, whose lives are vicious cycles of dreams, lies, and confessions, whereas others are made grotesque by their violent or macabre actions. Still others are so grotesquely limited that an alter ego is required for their completion. They are exemplified by the dual protagonists French Edward and Dr. Baby Levaster, characters first introduced in the early short stories and developed in *The Tennis Handsome,* a novella that, when compared with the first versions of its chapters, demonstrates the increasing poetic condensation characterizing Hannah's mature style. Hannah also extends his vision of the grotesque through fantastic or superhuman figures, such as the "grofft" and the legendary "yarp," the latter of which is the subject of what he calls his "riff" on the Arkansas mountain culture and Ozark folktales. Hannah's wide range of styles reflects influences from oral history and legend and from southern religious experience, as well as from the modernist literature of the absurd and postmodernism. Hannah's development is not so much from one of these traditions to another as it is toward a broader use of all traditions, with several often incorporated in the same work, one image or idiom humorously working against the grain of another. His almost Joycean intertextuality includes a multitude of allusions to, or parodies of, distinctive literary styles and individual works.

Hannah's techniques of comedy are inherited from the tall tale and other southern and southwestern traditions of humor, from the long history of satire, from modern existential traditions of dark humor, and from the carnivalesque. Like such writers as James Baldwin, Eudora Welty, and Fred Chappell, Hannah often expresses his unique comic vision through images of music. His tribute to the American frontier and to the romance of the Old West is illustrated most fully in the darkly comic *Never Die,* the novel that shows Hannah to be one of a number of contemporary writers fascinated with the West, possibly, as Robert Brinkmeyer thinks, as a way to explore masculinity, "away from the burden of southern history and southern women," as does, for example, Cormac McCarthy in *Blood Meridian, All the Pretty Horses,* and *The Crossing*—in effect, to "light out for the Territory," as Huck Finn does at the end of Twain's novel.[2]

In addition to these thematic issues, this book is concerned with the narrative techniques Hannah employs to establish his themes. Since *Geronimo Rex* and *Nightwatchmen,* Hannah has not written anything that looks like a traditional novel, either in length or in narrative structure. In fact, reviewers of his books continually speak of his fiction as both structurally and thematically chaotic, discontinuous, and fragmented, traits that link it with contemporary experiments in metafiction, although its relationship to oral tradition and to mainstream romantic and modernist literary traditions is undeniable. Contemporary short story theory seems especially amenable to describing the structures and rhythms of Hannah's fiction, both his short stories and his novellas. Two theoretical approaches to literature that are particularly useful in understanding some of the intricacies of his complicated narratives are those of literary recalcitrance and of a narrative rhythm that results from a plot's continuing past possible preclosure points and thus signifying in unexpected ways in narratives that at first may seem incoherent.

The world's first short story theorist, Edgar Allan Poe, did not insist that a short story have a coherent plot to achieve a single unified effect; nevertheless, as Thomas M. Leitch argues, short story readers trained in the Joycean mode of the epiphanic ending have come to expect at least some meaningful revelation at closure, a revelation that is often the result of a coherent move from innocence to knowledge. But in an alternate tradition, the nar-

---

2. Brinkmeyer, "Beyond the Veranda"; Mark Twain, *Adventures of Huckleberry Finn,* ed. Sculley Bradley, Richmond Croom Beatty, and E. Hudson Long (New York, 1962), 226.

rative rhythm moves toward a conclusion that debunks some illusions about what the story had led the reader to expect, as does Hemingway's "A Clean Well-Lighted Place" and Henry James's "The Figure in the Carpet." Barry Hannah's short fiction not only negates the illusion of the formal unity of story, with a tidy resolution at closure and thus the illusion of story as coherent mimesis in any traditional sense; it also destroys the illusion of the unitary self depicted by story and the Joycean illusion of the writer as a distant, disinterested creator. Hannah's four short story collections (*Airships, Captain Maximus, Bats Out of Hell,* and *High Lonesome*) all demonstrate these debunking characteristics, as do his short novels (*Ray, The Tennis Handsome, Hey Jack!, Boomerang,* and *Never Die*). One result of this kind of story is that in spite of its very real narrative intent, that is, its wish to tell a story, each narrative eschews a *single* story with a single theme, a practice that ignores Poe's dictum of the single effect. Hannah's fiction resembles what Ian Reid has called an "unstable area of textual play." As such, it includes multiple instances of intertextual borrowing as well as intergeneric structures, such as internal and/or external frame tales. Often a story is, in Reid's words, "a meetingplace for various generic tendencies." Moreover, not only Hannah's short stories but also his short novels are characterized by the debunking technique, which supports Leitch's contention that this nonepiphanic form of short story has influenced the still-dominant brief lyric mode of the American novel, as indeed the form also marks the works of such European novelists as Laurence Sterne and André Gide. Longer works marked by the debunking rhythm are "nonnovelistic novels," Leitch argues, because their "linear structure is obscure, [their] imagined world is unusually thin or [their] compass of time unusually short, and [their] unity is equivocal."[3]

In his essay "The Debunking Rhythm of the American Short Story," collected in the excellent book *Short Story Theory at a Crossroads,* Leitch examines American short story traditions, first differentiating between anecdotal (mimetic) stories, in which a closing revelation is based on external plot actions, and epiphanic (lyric) stories, in which a closing revelation is based on internal changes in character. The lyric short story, as theorist

3. Ian Reid, "Destabilizing Frames for Story," in *Short Story Theory at a Crossroads,* ed. Susan Lohafer and Jo Ellyn Clarey (Baton Rouge, 1989), 302–309; Thomas M. Leitch, "The Debunking Rhythm of the American Short Story," *ibid.,* 146.

Mary Rohrberger defines it, is characterized not by traditional plot structures but by "symbolic substructures, where patterning is defined by a principle of organization and where degrees of tensions or expectations and gratifications involve us in a steady rhythmic process toward a particular ending necessitated by the pattern involved." The lyric story can also be identified by what Austin M. Wright calls its "recalcitrance," that is, a built-in structure of obstacles to the quick comprehension of a story's meanings. This recalcitrance is achieved by such antimimetic techniques as radical juxtapositions of dissimilar narrative elements, rejection of overt action or of conventional beginnings and ends, and unresolved contradictions, all of which are also characteristics of metafiction, commonly known as postmodernist fiction, and sometimes surfiction.[4]

Recalcitrance is closely related to *reticence,* a term that Eudora Welty uses to discuss stories that are "opaque by reason of [an author's] intention," she says, citing the subtleties of, for example, Ernest Hemingway, Virginia Woolf, and William Faulkner. Welty herself, one of the world's finest practitioners of the "reticent" or "recalcitrant" short story and novella, points out that the "ordering" of a story's structure, which may seem obscure at first, is basic to both the beauty of the story and the reader's understanding of the writer:

> We have observed that the finest story writers seem to be in one sense obstructionists. . . . What is stranger is that if we look for the source of the deepest pleasure we receive from a writer, how often do we not find that it seems to be connected with this very obstruction.
>
> The fact is, apparently, that in pressing to our source of pleasure we have entered into another world. We are speaking of beauty. And beauty is not a blatant or promiscuous or obvious quality; indeed, it is associated with reticence, with stubbornness, of a number of kinds. It arises somehow from a desire not to comply with what may be expected, but to act inevitably, as

4. Leitch, "The Debunking Rhythm of the American Short Story," 131–46; Mary Rohrberger, "Between Shadow and Act: Where Do We Go from Here?" in *Short Story Theory at a Crossroads,* ed. Lohafer and Clarey, 40; Austin M. Wright, "Recalcitrance in the Short Story," in *Short Story Theory at a Crossroads,* ed. Lohafer and Clarey, 124–28. On the lyric quality of Hannah's fiction, see, for example, Larry McCaffery and Sinda Gregory, "An Interview with Barry Hannah," in *Alive and Writing: Interviews with American Authors of the 1980s,* ed. McCaffery and Gregory (Urbana, Ill., 1987), 120–21.

long as some human truth is in sight, whatever that inevitability may call for. Beauty is not a means, not a way of furthering a thing in the world. It is a result; it belongs to ordering, to form, to aftereffect.[5]

The "human truth . . . in sight" in fiction characterized by such reticence is often one that Leitch points to when he argues that such stories "commonly debunk a particular subject: the concept of a public identity, a self that acts in such a knowable, deliberate way as to assert a stable, discrete identity." This "critique of the notion of a stable . . . identity," he says, is "a means to the author's unmaking, and the audience's unknowing, an active, determinate self that was only an illusion to begin with." Leitch's further premise, that the debunking rhythm of the American short story has defined the character of all American fiction, suggests an important connection to the literary mainstream for contemporary writers of this kind of story, including postmodernists like Barry Hannah.[6]

Hannah's short fiction exemplifies the antithetical mode of the lyric tradition: it debunks several closely related assumptions of the modern mimetic narrative in ways that distinguish it from the epiphanic lyric, by challenging the illusion of story as coherent mimesis. Initiation stories are natural vehicles for the debunking rhythm, as exemplified by Flaubert's *Sentimental Education* and Hawthorne's "My Kinsman, Major Molineux," in both of which, Leitch points out, the young protagonists "lose their ideals and illusions without gaining any compensating revelation . . . or [any] stable conception of the world or of one's public identity." Hannah has made such extensive use of this and related techniques that a knowledge of the underlying mechanics is a helpful key to the narrative logic of his stories. A further key is the recognition of Hannah's unique blending of postmodern irony and carnivalesque humor with the style, content, and perspective of certain aspects of the romantic *bildungsroman*. One aim of this book is to offer the first substantial estimate of Hannah's literary achievement to date; another is to enable his readers to better appreciate a fiction that is far more than a brilliant linguistic tour de force, a fiction that shows the contemporary human, especially the contemporary male, em-

5. Eudora Welty, *The Eye of the Story* (New York, 1978), 89, 105.

6. Leitch, "The Debunking Rhythm of the American Short Story," in *Short Story Theory at a Crossroads,* ed. Lohafer and Clarey, 133–34, 146.

broiled in all the desperate hilarity required to make a brave show—all the "raving on the heath"—to counter the "slings and arrows of outrageous fortune" in our time. I do not use the Shakespearean idiom lightly here: I see Barry Hannah as a truthteller whose protagonists are comic blends of the raving Lear and the jester, the latter enjoying the license to deliver unpopular human truths, delighting us in spite of ourselves.[7]

7. *Ibid.,* 133.

Romance and Rage in the American Man-Child

I was a mad boy, angry about everything except my trumpet, which
I played out of the open windows of my bedroom. I'd play in the air
and try to make something happen in vacant air. . . . My notes
pierced out in the air with a sweet revenge on reality.
            —Barry Hannah, *Boomerang*

Memory is a great artist. For every man and for every woman it
makes the recollection of his or her life a work of art and an unfaithful record.
            —André Maurois, *Aspects of Biography*

THE LITERARY THEME of the American dream-nightmare is rooted in the
ambivalent character of the young nation at its most fundamental levels:
the split between reason and irrationality, between the practical and
forward-looking spirit of mature Enlightenment wisdom and the romantic, guilt-ridden spirit of nostalgia for youthful innocence. Leslie Fiedler
explains the phenomenon in his *Love and Death in the American Novel*:

> Insofar as America is legendary, a fact of the imagination as well as one of
> history, it has been shaped by the ideals of the Age of Reason. . . .

But America is not exclusively the product of Reason—not even in the area of legend. Behind its neo-classical façade, ours is a nation sustained by a sentimental and Romantic dream, the dream of an escape from culture and a renewal of youth. . . .

The dream of the Republic is quite a different thing from that of the Revolution. The vision of blood and fire as ritual purification, the need to cast down what is up, to degrade the immemorial images of authority, to impose equality as the ultimate orthodoxy—these came from the *Encyclopédie*, perhaps, as abstract ideas; but the spirit in which they were lived was that of full-blown Romanticism . . . [with an underside of] profound inner insecurity and guilt, a hidden world of nightmare not abolished by manifestos or restrained by barricades. The final horrors, as modern society has come to realize, are neither gods nor demons, but intimate aspects of our own minds.[1]

This psychic split manifests itself throughout the major traditions of American literature, from Charles Brockden Brown and J. Fenimore Cooper onward, as Fiedler demonstrates. Its viability continues in contemporary literature, nowhere more clearly than in the fiction of Barry Hannah. In portrayals of the dreams, illusions, and nightmares of adolescents trying to achieve self-initiation into adult culture and of men at any age trying to come to terms with the cultural mythologies of war and heroes, Hannah extends the literary examination of the troubled psyche of the American male.

In Hannah's initiation stories, he writes out of and against the long and well-recognized tradition established by Cooper and continued by Nathaniel Hawthorne, Stephen Crane, Mark Twain, Sherwood Anderson, Ernest Hemingway, J. D. Salinger, Saul Bellow, and John Updike. Although Hannah is influenced by this tradition, he modifies it by his own version of another major literary genre, that of autobiography. Life writing also began early in the history of this country, with the diaries of William Bradford, John Winthrop, and the other founding colonists, and with spiritual autobiographies, such as that of Jonathan Edwards, the fiery preacher of the eighteenth-century religious revivalist movement known as the Great

1. Leslie Fiedler, *Love and Death in the American Novel* (Rev. ed.; New York, 1992), 36–38.

Awakening. These were soon followed by autobiographical accounts on the pattern of the European *bildungsroman,* beginning in adolescence and continuing throughout a career; the most celebrated account is undoubtedly Benjamin Franklin's.[2] In the late nineteenth century, autobiography based on the boyhood years alone developed into a genre that was not only popular but, according to William Dean Howells, potentially instrumental in the development of the American novel.

Howells' prediction is recalled by Marcia Jacobson in *Being a Boy Again: Autobiography and the American Boy Book,* which examines the most popular of the boy books—those of Thomas Bailey Aldrich, Charles Dudley Warner, Mark Twain, Hamlin Garland, Booth Tarkington, and Howells himself.[3] These fictionalized autobiographies were very different from the traditional notion of life writing, but they bear a close relation to Hannah's work, which also mixes fiction with personal history. Hannah's stories usually include characters representing both himself and his real-life acquaintances, some with actual or thinly disguised names. The experiences of his adolescents often parallel his own experiences growing up in Clinton, a small town west of Jackson, Mississippi, where he was born in 1942. As a teenager in the late 1950s, too small for the football team, he played trumpet in the high school band, as does his protagonist in *Boomerang.*

In most turn-of-the-century boy books, the age of the protagonist is between eight and twelve years; likewise, some of Hannah's characters are as young as eight and many others but a few years older. These and other striking similarities in both perspective and method between his fiction and the boy books urge consideration of his work in the light of that short-lived genre and of the broader, more venerable tradition of autobiography.

Like the boy books of a century ago, Hannah's stories are neither by nor for boys but are rather stories of a boy's life written by and for adult males. His stories are also for any reader who wants a frank look into the most imaginative of boy natures as depicted by a brilliant contemporary writer. Readers interested in the complexity of the male psyche will find that Hannah's fiction reveals some of the hilarious, engaging, reprehensible, and painful truths about adolescent and adult male dreams, fears, needs, and

2. *The Autobiography of Benjamin Franklin* (Philadelphia, 1964).

3. Marcia Jacobson, *Being a Boy Again: Autobiography and the American Boy Book* (Tuscaloosa, Ala., 1994), 1.

desires. For example, his stories highlight what Jacobson identifies in the boy books as the young boy's "love of fighting and self-display" but also his insecurity, his combination of "humiliation and sexual timidity"; in Hannah's fiction, as in the boy books, such vulnerabilities are commonly masked by humor. Like the authors of the boy books, Hannah imaginatively transforms autobiography to arrive at psychological rather than factual truth, often including passages of lyrical, and sometimes elegiac, beauty in his nostalgic re-creation of the scenes of youthful experiences.[4]

In his discussion of American literature's most famous boy book, Mark Twain's *Adventures of Huckleberry Finn,* Leslie Fiedler remarks on the "double truth fumbled by most other books on the subject: how truly wonderful it is to remember our childhood; and yet how we cannot recall it without revealing to ourselves the roots of the very terror, which in adulthood has driven us nostalgically to evoke that past." The author of a turn-of-the-century boy book often was responding to a crisis in his adult life in which he found himself wanting in some respect; and in the resulting narrative (or narratives, in the case of those who wrote sequels or series of books) based on his boyhood, the author often depicted a confrontation with a less-than-satisfactory or absent father. Since the most pervasive theme in Hannah's stories is that of the mixed blessings of boyhood, or of the ambivalent maturity of boyishly insecure adult males trying to emulate what Fiedler calls "the Good Bad Boy," the stories can be seen as boy books for the last decades of the twentieth century.[5]

In the process of describing the boy book genre—more properly, a subgenre of autobiography—that developed from the late nineteenth to the early twentieth century, Jacobson notes the influence of the "recapitulation theory," a psychological notion current at the time that held that the development of boys between the ages of eight and twelve was analogous to that of the human species: young boys are essentially savages who must be encouraged to express and not repress this nature before they are ready for civilized adult life. The theory maintained that society would ultimately transform uncivilized boys in a way much like the "miraculous conversion of sinners." The logical fallacy in this pre-Freudian theory is that it ignored

4. *Ibid.,* 24, 39, 52–53, 138–41, 151, 153–54.
5. Fiedler, *Love and Death in the American Novel,* 289.

a cultural truth about the ordinarily repressed and often thinly veiled incivility of male adults, whose true nature was revealed, Jacobson states, not only in the brutality of the Civil War but also in the unconscionable treatment of Native Americans and even in everyday cutthroat business practices. Howells and others, she points out, realized that the recapitulation theory "comfortably obscured the central fact of everyday adult male life in the period . . . that it was in fact boyhood savagery writ large." That the theory was generally accepted and thus that adult men read the boy books with avid nostalgia, secure in the illusion that their boyish savagery was sealed in the past, "reminds us," Jacobson says, "how adept Americans are at denying unpleasant truths about themselves."[6]

In Hannah's fiction, this tacit cultural conspiracy to ignore or misrepresent the male nature, and the alternating denial and admission of the lie, provide a major source of dramatic tension. The lie as trope is often used to demonstrate the author's experience of it as a many-faceted cultural betrayal, such as that related by Hannah when Jan Nordby Gretlund interviewed him in 1984. Asked about his religious beliefs, for example, Hannah replied, "If I said that I believed in God, what would it mean? I proceed from the fact that there has been a great lie to me, from the word go. Somebody stands in the pulpit and says, 'I've just talked to God.' You get a little lonely when you realize that's not right, at about sixteen. There's something too frantic about the present religious fervor, especially on TV." This oblique response to Gretlund's question, with its jump-cut to the idea of a perceived "great lie" that Hannah apparently takes personally, suggests one of the pervasive themes in a fiction that, Hannah says, is concerned with "finding and asking the big questions." It also echoes the sentiment of J. D. Salinger's Holden Caulfield, the adolescent protagonist of *The Catcher in the Rye,* who "like[s] Jesus and all" but who "can't . . . stand ministers [because] they sound so phony when they talk."[7]

Ironically, many of Hannah's characters are themselves liars who suffer from the perception that some "great lie" has been perpetrated against them. They seem to be caught in a double bind of causes and effects that,

6. Jacobson, *Being a Boy Again,* 15.

7. Jan Nordby Gretlund, "Barry Hannah," *Contemporary Authors,* Vol. CX, ed. Hal May (Detroit, 1984), 235; J. D. Salinger, *The Catcher in the Rye* (1951; rpr. New York, 1979), 99–100.

when aggravated by the specifically gender-based, culturally predicated dreams and burdens of contemporary boys and men, often leads to grotesque attempts to live a meaningful existence. The dreams of Hannah's male characters taunt them, often inciting them to a violence that requires expiation; but there is no religious expiation for them. They are in some ways as "lonely" as the author claimed to be; and lacking a religious means of confession, they indulge in secular rituals of confession that alternate with dreams and lies in vicious circles and other patterns that provide coherent narrative structure to a fiction that appears on its surface to be the epitome of postmodern fragmentation.

The "great lie," as treated in Hannah's fiction, is more general than the specific lie about religion of which Hannah complained to Gretlund; it may include all the lies our culture has told us and that we have told and continue to tell about ourselves and to ourselves, especially about the reality of the natures of men, women, and children. Even the child in Hannah's fiction, who clearly is the father of the man, lies. In the autobiographical fantasy *Boomerang*, the child narrator lies as he tries to rationalize his violence against the "preacher's kids . . . [who were] so poor they had to eat cold cereal for lunch." They were, he says, "horrible skinny people with bad complexions," a childish remark he immediately counters with, "That's not true. That's a hideous statement. They were good and swift, and they were mean. We fought them with mudballs and threw cane spears at them. They were down there beyond the tall cane patch and they had nothing to eat and we were glad" (2–3). And the same kind of wish-fulfillment discourse obtains at the end of the novel, when the same character, now an adult, says, "After three years of trying my wife and I have a new baby coming," followed by, "What a lie. We have nothing coming" (148). This passage also echoes the disillusionment of Salinger's Holden, who finds almost everyone but his little sister "phony." Wandering alone in New York's Central Park after flunking out of prep school, Holden thinks, "It didn't seem at all like Christmas was coming soon. It didn't seem like *anything* was coming."[8]

Hannah's fiction confronts the painful reality of the cultural great lie through the stories of individual liars; yet the lies are constantly countered by the dream that is at the heart of American life and literature. Joyce Carol

8. Salinger, *Catcher in the Rye*, 117–18, Salinger's emphasis.

Oates asserts that American literature from the beginning reflects the fact that Americans "seek the absolute dream." As Gary Waller has said of Oates's fiction, so it may be said of Hannah's: the lies experienced by the fictional characters all point to "the tragic gaps between word and act, ideal and reality—not in a trivial everyday sense but almost as a metaphysical principle, felt the more strongly just because we are seekers of meaning, not merely of contentment." Hannah's fiction is played out in those gaps; the actions of his characters are all in some sense like those of the young trumpet player in *Boomerang,* whose music is an attempt to "make something happen in vacant air [that is] a sweet revenge on reality" (17), or, as Jacobson remarks of Twain's Tom Sawyer, to act out of an "imperious imagination that redeems mundane life." Booth Tarkington's narrator articulates the same principle, as he describes Penrod's fourth-grade days: "The nervous monotony of the schoolroom inspires a sometimes unbearable longing for something astonishing to happen . . . , [thus] every boy's fundamental desire is to do something astonishing himself, so as to be the centre of all human interest and awe." In literary-critical terms, this need to "make something happen" or "do something astonishing" is what Peter Brooks has called the desire that propels a narrative, a desire that "drives the protagonist forward . . . [in such a way that] the ambitious hero thus stands as a figure of the reader's efforts to construct meanings." This theory of narrative desire involves a reader-response technique that derives from Freud's concept, in *Beyond the Pleasure Principle,* of desire as a force, and from post-structuralist applications of this psychoanalytic theory to the dynamics of the written narrative, especially applications by Jacques Lacan in *Ecrits* and by Jacques Derrida in *Figures III.*[9]

Like the boy books, which are, Jacobson says, "not about growing up, but . . . instead about the meaning of boyhood for the adult author," Hannah's fiction simply presents more than it develops character. David Madden, a fine writer himself, even as he praised Hannah's brilliant style in *Ge-*

---

9. Joyce Carol Oates, *The Edge of Impossibility: Tragic Forms in Literature* (New York, 1972), 3; Gary F. Waller, *Dreaming America: Obsession and Transcendence in the Fiction of Joyce Carol Oates* (Baton Rouge, 1979), 31; Jacobson, *Being a Boy Again,* 44. Tarkington's "A Boy in the Air," as serialized in *Cosmopolitan* in 1913, is quoted in Jacobson, *Being a Boy Again,* 144. Peter Brooks, *Reading for the Plot: Design and Intention in Narrative* (New York, 1984), 39.

ronimo Rex, objected to the lack of development in Harry Monroe, the protagonist of this novel. More than twenty years later, however, Hannah continues to write linguistically and structurally brilliant stories and novels in which the creation of mostly flat (nondeveloping, certainly not dull!) characters continues to be a narrative technique of choice. Hannah's affinity for the short story and the episodic novella may contribute to this propensity; but Hannah may also be reflecting, perhaps unconsciously, what Edwin H. Cady, in his definition of the boy book, called "an imaginative exploration of the nature and predicament of the man-child." In other words, Hannah's choice of what E. M. Forster called the "flat character" may be a realistic technique that reflects an actual lack of development in the adult male, who is at heart but a boy. Thus, Hannah's fiction seems to confirm Howells' contention that the fierce conflicts between modern labor and modern capital were only another phase of boyhood savagery: that only the methods of savagery change as the boy grows toward manhood. Often, the "boy" seems to surface in the man in matters of sex and other areas where a certain level of performance is expected, and where, as a result, his performance may range anywhere between boyish savagery and boyish enthusiasm. Age, then, as an indicator of maturity, self-confidence, and power, is an important subject throughout Hannah's work, and is often suggested by the voice, which identifies whether one is "manly" and certain other aspects of character. Once a reader is aware of the importance of the theme of age and aging, even an ostensibly offhand comment takes on more significance, for example, Thorpe Trove's self-correction in *Nightwatchmen,* when he describes a college student as "a man, or old boy" (*N,* 6). In that novel—Hannah's only murder mystery—when Trove's Aunt Glory dies, the doctor who attends her in the hospital emergency room, and who had apparently once loved her, "had the almost mystic look of a mad adolescent . . . [with] a frightening boyish striving in his face" as he looks at her (20). In the world of Hannah's fiction, all situations involving the opposite sex seem to reduce men to boys, full of "striving" but without mature means of expression or action.[10]

10. Jacobson, *Being a Boy Again,* 4; Madden, "Barry Hannah's *Geronimo Rex* in Retrospect," 316; Edwin H. Cady, *The Road to Realism: The Early Years, 1837–1885, of William Dean Howells* (Syracuse, 1956), 12; E. M. Forster, *Aspects of the Novel* (1927; rpr. New York, 1954).

"Boyish striving" that is "frightening," as in the case of the doctor in *Nightwatchmen,* is the aberrant feature of Hannah's adolescents, characterizing almost every encounter they have with other life, human or animal. In *Geronimo Rex,* for the eight-year-old third-grader Harriman Monroe, whose mind is "full of little else but notes on the atrocities of World War II," violence is a way of life. He plays at shooting his air rifle at "Jap snipers" who might be hiding in the cane patch, and he takes deadly aim with a hickory stick at a peacock that has not only attacked and terrified him but also humiliated him by booby-trapping his play area with dung:

> I hit a dip and slid off into that peafowl dung I didn't know was there. It was all in my hair and up the barrel of my gun, and my lever had this unmentionable stalactite of green hanging on it. I looked around and saw there wouldn't be any decent playing in here until maybe I was twenty. . . . I stood still and swung on the peacock with both arms. I caught him on the head, and his beak swerved like plastic. He dropped on the bricks like a club, his fantail all folded in. I toed him. He was dead, with an eye wiped away. (19)

When his father threatens corporal punishment for his killing of their well-off neighbor's bird, Harry retains enough bravado from the experience to avoid a thrashing by astonishing his father with the practical suggestion to destroy the evidence with lime. Harry knows that lime will quickly eat away the flesh of the peacock's carcass, because "the Nazis used it on bodies in concentration camps" (20).

As a teenager, Harry changes the weapons and the motivation for violence. He shoots a pistol at an unsuspecting organist whose playing of the "triumphant" music of Bach has annoyed him and has also seemed to mock Zak, Harry's feckless college drama teacher, who has been less than triumphant in attempted lovemaking with his fiancée, the wheelchair-bound Linda. Even a week later, Harry feels elated by his use of the gun, which he carries in imitation of his hero, the Apache Geronimo. As he tries to convince Zak that he shot the organist because Zak and Linda were in danger—a patently "false cause"—he deliberately prolongs the mental exhilaration of his bravado by pretending that the organist "was not harmless." He confesses, "My mind pounded, for the first time in my life, as if it was a thing distinct from me, and in my body I experienced cold sprays of nerves. Life shot through me as if existence really meant something. Before pulling the trigger in the auditorium, I seemed to be only verging toward life—say, like a man eating color photographs. But now the excitement was hounding me" (*GR,* 164). Thus, Harry is motivated by a combination of fearful "cold sprays of nerves" and the thrill of shooting the gun. As Hannah explained to Scott Cawelti, "It's in the French mode . . . creating art by drawing a pistol. You know, it's the absolute act, the act of firing a gun randomly into a crowd—it's the absolute act of art . . . your existential act."[11]

Hannah is not alone among southern writers who create characters that live vicariously through some fantasy world of excitement or that generate extravagant situations to heighten the mundane reality of their lives. Whether by direct influence or merely the fact of kindred authorial spirits, Hannah's Harry Monroe seems to echo, even to the trope of the photographs, the existentialist sentiments of Walker Percy's Binx Bolling, especially in the depiction of a mental state in which "life shot through [Harry] as if existence really meant something," compared with one in which he "seemed to be only verging toward life." Many of Percy's protagonists scorn those who seem to have chosen "everydayness" or "careers of the commonplace." In *The Moviegoer,* Binx tries to avoid the "abyss" of existential "despair" by living vicariously, interpreting life through the movies; and Kate wants to "break out of dead center." For Binx, the cinema's larger-than-life "ghosts of heroes are more real" than the people he knows. In Percy's *Lancelot,* the title character is in a fight for personal survival that will enable him, like a grail knight, to bring "life to a dead land."[12]

Because outraged characters commit outrageous, larger-than-life actions that take "a sweet revenge on reality" in Hannah's fiction (*B,* 17), and because these actions usually involve sex, violence, and humor, reviewers and other commentators, such as John Skow, Larry McCaffery and Sinda Gregory, and Daniel Marowski, often place his work in some relation to the Southern Gothic, especially to the fiction of Flannery O'Connor. But such attributions of influence are misleadingly simplistic: whereas O'Connor's fiction points to an orthodox (Roman Catholic) Christian moral, Hannah's focuses on a more secular aspect of the nature of the human self and on the

11. Scott Cawelti, "An Interview with Barry Hannah," *Short Story,* n.s., III (1995), 107.

12. Walker Percy, *The Moviegoer* (1961; rpr. New York, 1989), 133, 9, 97, 159; Percy, *Lancelot* (1977; rpr. New York, 1980), 8.

aesthetic question of how best to—indeed, whether one can—write that self. Early on, Michael Malone found that in *Airships,* Hannah was "more secular and less furious than O'Connor"; despite a significant concern with religious faith that has continued in later books, and regardless of the rage expressed by many Hannah characters, Malone's statement remains essentially valid. Although Hannah's connection with the Gothic tradition of the comic grotesque is undeniable, O'Connor writes of a nongendered spiritual illness through mostly female viewpoints, whereas Hannah describes symptoms of a contemporary and particularly masculine malaise. Consonant with contemporary genre theory, which argues that an autobiographer writes to create a "self," Hannah seems to be not only creating the selves of his fictional characters but also creating or re-creating himself as he writes. In essence, in each fiction he imagines what James Olney has described as a "new self, which is born in the moment now out of this very exercise of consciousness and memory." Perhaps, as Ihab Hassan has said of Norman Mailer, Hannah needs "to create a Legend in order to live—with danger, with generosity, with rage—and so create the Work. . . . What if the [writer] required a fiction to include himself . . . (Author plus Man)?" Merely the titles of stories like "Midnight and I'm Not Famous Yet," a story from *Airships,* suggest such a need, without detracting in the least from the complex significance of the total work.[13]

Hannah's relation to the Gothic is more aptly to the Gothic sense that Joyce Carol Oates describes, in her own use of it, as "a fairly realistic assessment of modern life." It bespeaks a sense of being as lost in the world as in the labyrinth of a Gothic castle, but the key that Hannah's characters are searching for is to the puzzle of themselves. They, like Oates's protagonists, are "haunted" by contemporary versions of the original American dream, which persists as an absolute dream of fulfillment, of significance, of meaning. As Oates says, "The crudity of our desire [is not only] for an absolute

13. John Skow, Review of *Geronimo Rex,* in the Washington *Post,* April 19, 1972; McCaffery and Gregory, "An Interview with Barry Hannah," 4, 111; Daniel Marowski, "Barry Hannah," in *Contemporary Literary Criticism,* ed. Marowski, XXXVIII (Detroit, 1986), 231; Michael Malone, "Everything That Rises," Review of *Airships,* in *Nation,* June 10, 1978, p. 706; James Olney, *Metaphors of Self: The Meaning of Autobiography* (Princeton, 1972), 25; Ihab Hassan, "Focus on Norman Mailer's *Why Are We in Vietnam?*" in *American Dreams, American Nightmares,* ed. David Madden (Carbondale, Ill., 1970), 197.

dream [but also for] an absolute key." The universal need for the "curve of devastation and elevation" that comes to the tragic hero in literature is a vicarious experience, she says, that provides us with the hope that meaning exists. Of our appropriation of such hope, Oates explains, "The hero dies into our imaginations as we, helplessly, live out lives that are never works of art—even the helpless lives of 'artists'!—and are never understood. Suffering is articulated in tragic literature, and so this literature is irresistible, a therapy of the soul. We witness in art the reversal of our commonplace loss of passion, our steady loss of consciousness that is never beautiful but only biological." Thus the more profound link between the characters of Hannah and O'Connor is not the Gothic; rather, it is the same as that between the characters of Hannah and Oates: a common yearning after an absolute. In fact, Hannah often parodies the Gothic. When John Griffin Jones asked whether the Southern Gothic tradition was "something that [Hannah] wanted to work against," he responded, "Yes. I use it. I think it's a wonderful background for all kinds of farce." He cited the "spooky old house that Whitfield Peter lives in . . . [which is] a fraud, a complete phoney [with] all the old vines everywhere [in *Geronimo Rex*]."[14]

Hannah's characters often seem to inhabit a moral void that is the secular version of what Robert Brinkmeyer describes as "the absence of sacramental vision in modern consciousness" in O'Connor's depiction. Unlike O'Connor, however, Hannah creates no fatuous Hulgas or Mrs. Turpins who must be chastised by divine epiphanies of violence; similarly, there are no characters like Welty's Laurel McKelva Hand, protagonist of *The Optimist's Daughter,* who must be jolted into an awareness of bondage to the past. Instead, Hannah's characters demonstrate an incipient moral consciousness because they already know, as the narrator-protagonist of *Ray* says, that "something's wrong" (102). Their eagerness to confess their culpability modifies the comic grotesque and thus further complicates the task of assigning genre to works already problematical because of their mixing of real and fictional characters and events. Like Oates's characters, Han-

14. Oates, quoted in "Joyce Carol Oates: Writing as a Natural Reaction," *Time,* October 10, 1969, p. 108; Oates, *The Edge of Impossibility,* 4. It is perhaps not beside the point that Oates takes the phrase "the absolute dream" from absurdist dramatist Eugène Ionesco's *Fragments of a Journal,* a long excerpt of which serves as the epigraph to her book. John Griffin Jones, "Barry Hannah," in *Mississippi Writers Talking,* ed. Jones (Jackson, Miss., 1982), 142.

nah's are caught in a no-man's land, somewhere between tragic stature and the helplessness of "lives that are never works of art"; obsessed with the absolute dream of a wished-for *truth,* they are thwarted at every turn by lies. Indeed, their seeming helplessness is deepened by their suspicion that the dream itself is a lie, because they, the dreamers, are great liars. The similarity between Oates's and Hannah's thematic structures is remarkable, for her characters also are obsessed by dreams that contain the seeds of self-betrayal and thus turn into nightmares. Hannah's concern is not primarily with the rampant materialism that defeats many of Oates's protagonists but with a more personal agony, a psychological counterpart of the biological loss that makes Grandma Wendall, for example, in Oates's *Them,* "baffled at the failure of her body to keep up with her assessment of herself."[15]

Hannah creates mostly male protagonists, and the dream of which he writes is the particular dream of the "macho" male in American culture. It is a dream not only of achievement but also of heroism, not only of love but of sexual dominance, too. Yet the critical tensions in his fiction come not so much from any outside human or environmental antagonist as from the protagonist's psyche. One reason for this self-antagonism is that Hannah's adult male characters live in an age that is conscious of feminist politics. They are sensitive but ambivalent idealists who would like to live out an absolute dream that, when they will admit it to themselves, they know is amoral, often immoral, and unfailingly sexist. Indeed, their consciences tell them that their dream is based on cultural falsehoods that they have internalized. One such falsehood, evidence of which Allen Shepherd has observed in Hannah's "Water Liars," is "the vaguely feministic idea that many men have trouble accommodating women's sexuality, licit or illicit."[16]

This dual theme of dreams and lies emerges from a fiction that never allows the reader to forget the author's presence, not only because the narrative voice is so intimate but also because the author makes explicit statements of literary aesthetics and thematics. Thus the narrative has the double-voiced perspective that allowed the authors of the nineteenth-

15. Robert H. Brinkmeyer, Jr., *The Art and Vision of Flannery O'Connor* (Baton Rouge, 1989), 2; Joyce Carol Oates, *Them* (Greenwich, Conn., 1969), 90.

16. Allen Shepherd, "Outrage and Speculation: Barry Hannah's *Airships,*" *Notes on Mississippi Writers,* XIV (1982), 66.

century boy books to achieve ironic distance from the traumas of their boy-hood. The characteristic methods by which Hannah achieves a similar ironic distance are constant authorial references to writing; writer-characters who comment on their work; puns in the dialogue; and a narrative rhythm that supports Hannah's debunking of cultural myths, including myths about gender. Two significant examples of authorial statements are from "Testimony of Pilot": "It was talent to keep the metronome ticking amidst any given chaos of sound" (*A*, 28); "Memory, the whole lying opera of it, is killing me now" (*A*, 32). Hannah writes about the American male's individual and lonely search for an absolute dream of manly behavior among cultural memories and expectations that continually betray him. The narrative rhythm achieved by his characters' vacillating preoccupations with the dream, the cultural lie, and their obsessive need to confess their complicity in the process constitutes a "metronome ticking" throughout "the whole lying opera" of Hannah's fiction.

The contemporary dilemma of Hannah's anxious protagonists is suggested by their description of themselves in alternately macho-heroic and self-deprecatory, often adolescent, terms of gendered expectations that have long been the subject of social science research. In 1963, the problem for males was stated this way:

> In an important sense there is only one complete unblushing male in America: a young, married, white, urban, northern, heterosexual Protestant father of college education, fully employed, of good complexion, weight, and height, and a recent record in sports. Every American male tends to look out upon the world from this perspective, this constituting one sense in which one can speak of a common value system in America. Any male who fails to qualify in any one of these ways is likely to view himself—during moments at least—as unworthy, incomplete, and inferior.[17]

From his earliest to his most recent stories, Hannah has demonstrated his fascination with adolescence. When John Updike identified the protagonist of *Geronimo Rex* as a new, "whining" Holden Caulfield, he seemed not far off the mark. Given Hannah's representation in subsequent fiction

17. Erving Goffman, *Stigma: Notes on the Management of Spoiled Identity* (Englewood Cliffs, N.J., 1963), 128.

of what is essentially this same character—who, like Holden, is continually outraged by human "phoniness"—Updike's evaluation now seems simplistic. The existentially disillusioned Harry Monroe of *Geronimo Rex* may be seen as the prototype of other Hannah protagonists: Ned Maximus, for example, in *Captain Maximus,* who not only sees life's fraudulence in "Dallas, city of the fur helicopters" but also knows that he himself is a fraud and a liar (39). And the violent expressions of power that David Madden describes as Monroe's "adolescent techniques for mental survival" in *Geronimo Rex* are similar to those of the young characters of *Boomerang,* who are "tiny but . . . sincere" (*B,* 1), and to those of *Captain Maximus,* who perceive themselves to be "swift fodder for the others" (*CM,* 58).[18]

That Hannah is still concerned with adolescent initiation in *Bats Out of Hell* is apparent in "Nicodemus Bluff," a story selected by Anne Tyler for inclusion in Shannon Ravenel's collection of the South's best short stories published from 1986 to 1995. It presents a parody of that quintessential southern story of a boy's initiation into manhood—Faulkner's "The Bear." The narrator of "Nicodemus Bluff," Harris Greeves, looks back from midlife on the events that transpired when he was the ten-year-old "little Harris" who had been allowed to accompany a group of men to a deer camp in Arkansas. The men do hardly any hunting, since it rains almost constantly during the days at camp, but a lot goes on in the mind of little Harris as he watches his father's obsessive behavior, including a bizarre personality change (wherein the elder Greeves becomes possessed by an aggressive female spirit and voice) during a marathon chess game that is somehow re- lated to satisfying Gomar Greeves's business debts to his opponent, Garrand Pool. In this story of nineteen pages, Hannah manages to include the themes of initiation and of the relations between races, classes, genders, and generations. In addition, contemporary problems—drugs, war, corruption in business, and sin in general—are raised.[19]

Harris Greeves begins his narration by confessing that as a college student his drug abuse often rendered him unable to tell whether he was "in church or jail" and by implying that his habit had been brought on by the

18. John Updike, "From Dyna Domes to Turkey-Pressing," Review of *Geronimo Rex,* in *New Yorker,* September 9, 1972, p. 124; Madden, "Barry Hannah's *Geronimo Rex* in Retrospect," 311.

19. Shannon Ravenel, ed., *Best of the South: From Ten Years of "New Stories from the South,"* selected by Anne Tyler (Chapel Hill, 1996).

memory of the trauma he suffered during that fateful trip to the deer camp, compounded by his father's death soon after. "Something happened when I was out there," Harris relates. "My father died that next week, but even so he still seemed to hang at the border of my space—the bars, the church window, that ten-foot cube—bloody and broken up and flattened in the nose, a black bruise on his cheekbone because of what happened to him with those others years ago down in the swamps" (*BOH,* 363). The catalyst for the present narrative is apparently Harris' treatment by a psychoanalyst, since he confesses that "it was tough and deep, but in talking it up Dr. Debord believed I would get better and be about my work at the animal shelter" (364). Both the psychological content and the language of the story have a clear connection to the wider scope of Faulkner's fiction, especially to the deep insecurities that lead to Quentin Compson's suicide in *Absalom, Absalom!* In "Nicodemus Bluff," the associational logic in Harris' meditation—on "why we had a nice house, lawn, two cars, even a yard man who rode a riding mower, a Negro named Whit who was nice to me"—begins with the memory of Whit's cutting himself and Harris' speculation that the Negro's "blood might be bluer [than his own]," and it leads to Harris' self-questioning: "Why do people live here at all, I ask. They must know this is a filthy, wrong, haunted place. Even the trees that are left look wrong or wronged, beat up. The red dirt is hopeless. The squirrels are thin and there is much—you can't get around it—suicide on the part of possums, coons, armadillos and deer who tried to exist in the puny scratch but could not, deciding then to leap out on the highway. There are no stories of any merit to come out of this place" (364–65). The passage parodies Shreve's demand of Quentin Compson: "Tell about the South. What's it like there. What do they do there. Why do they live there. Why do they live at all." As Louis D. Rubin, Jr., remarks, "Faulkner chose Quentin Compson, because Quentin embodied that aspect of his own imagination that could look at slavery, racism, noblesse oblige, the Confederate cause, the ambition of a poor white to become a planter, the class structure, openly and honestly." "Nicodemus Bluff" is one of the stories in which Hannah takes a brief, humorous, but serious critical look at some of these same problems, which have long burdened the South.[20]

20. William Faulkner, *Absalom, Absalom!* (1936; rpr. New York, 1951), 174; Louis D. Rubin, Jr., *The Mockingbird in the Gum Tree: A Literary Gallimaufry* (Baton Rouge, 1991), 53.

One of Hannah's most obvious connections to Faulkner's fiction is to the theme of rage, which is established by the propensity toward unfocused violence because of some grievance against the world. As Faulkner demonstrates throughout his fiction, such a propensity is one of the few characteristics not limited to any age, race, class, or gender. In *Absalom, Absalom!*, it is expressed, for example, by Quentin as he speculates about Miss Rosa Coldfield's "incredulous and unbearable amazement . . . [at] blind circumstance and savage event . . . [followed by] the lonely thwarted old female flesh embattled for forty-three years in the old insult, the old unforgiving outraged and betrayed by the final complete affront which was Sutpen's death." And it is not only Miss Rosa's rage Quentin describes; it is a more general malaise, which also affects him, so that even as he tells Shreve about it, far removed in the New England winter, he "seem[s] to hear the single profound suspiration of the parched earth's agony rising toward the imponderable and aloof stars." He is describing, in near-naturalistic terms, the rage of puny creatures in a cold and hostile universe.[21]

It is expressed most poignantly in Faulkner's symbolic "boy at the door," the most salient examples of which are Thomas Sutpen in *Absalom, Absalom!* and Sarty Snopes in "Barn Burning," both of whom feel betrayed by their fathers of low class and low standards, who brought them into a grossly unequal world at an insurmountable disadvantage. These characters seem doomed to resort to violence, enraged at their powerlessness to counter the scandal of everyday life, a scandal that continually profanes the Edenic or heroic dream. Young Sutpen, for example, has his innocence shattered when, being sent to the plantation manor house "on business, in the good faith of business which he had believed that all men accepted . . . he [is] told to go around to the back door even before he could state his errand." In his astonishment at being thus dismissed, and no less astonished by "the very broadcloth and linen and silk stockings the monkey nigger stood in to tell him," all he can think is, "But I can shoot him." Hannah brings Faulkner's theme of rage into the late twentieth century. In *Boomerang,* mistakenly thinking he has found a hero in an eighty-four-year-old homeless black man who "looks like a man floating on serene thoughts after his immense history of thinking and deciding," Hannah's child protag-

---

21. Faulkner, *Absalom, Absalom!*, 14, 362.

onist wants to "take him some food and offer my respects." But the illusion that he has found a hero-mentor is destroyed when he hears that the old man carries a gun; thus, the boy realizes, "He's just as scared as the rest of us" (11–12). To be sure, despite the Enlightenment rhetoric of the Revolution, the archetypes that have shaped the American male's understanding of heroism are not those characterized by "thinking and deciding." On the contrary, aggression, often with automatic weapons, is commonly seen as the means of choice for overcoming fear and assuming power, a fact that seems to support the conclusion of social scientists Robert Woolfolk and Frank Richardson that "the birthright of every American male is a chronic sense of personal inadequacy."[22]

Under traditional conventions, according to Joseph H. Pleck, masculinity is validated by "individual physical strength and aggression" and by invulnerability, especially to emotions, whereas modern males are validated by "economic achievement and organizational or bureaucratic power." Although moderns began to value emotional sensitivity, Pleck finds that well into the 1980s it was common to think it should occur "only with women." In a reevaluation of what heroism should entail, Mark Gerzon lists the frontiersman, the soldier, the breadwinner, the expert, and the lord as symbols of manhood that were "once useful . . . [because] they promised survival and well-being." Gerzon believes that although men have been well able to adjust to contemporary technological changes, somehow they have not been able to accommodate themselves to the lack of need for those traits that once were considered heroic against a human or environmental life-threatening enemy. Moreover, Gerzon argues, not only have traditional images become problematic or invalid, as has that of John Wayne, but the entire issue has been complicated by the women's movement. It may be most complicated for the man who, in spite of himself, clings to outdated ideas of what is heroic or manly and yet has no peace because he knows these images are not productive. The resulting dilemma provides enough models in the society at large to account for the savage, dysfunctional nature of Hannah's characters. Hannah himself points to "something inside of the male body [that makes him] want to run, hit, do something with this great

22. *Ibid.*, 233–34; Robert L. Woolfolk and Frank C. Richardson, *Sanity, Stress, and Survival* (New York, 1978), 57.

amount of muscle frame you're given [that makes men continue to act as] hunter and gatherer . . . [because] you're not supposed to sit around looking at a Smith-Corona typing." Hannah, like Faulkner, knows that these feelings become an inevitable part of a writer's fiction. Admitting this autobiographical aspect of *The Sound and the Fury,* Faulkner explained that "because it is himself the Southern writer is writing about, the writer unconsciously writes into every line and phrase his violent despairs and rages and frustrations or his violent prophesies of still more violent hopes."[23]

A continuing theme in Hannah's fiction is that of the contrast between intellectual power and violence; it voices the autobiographical truth of Hannah's conflict between his vocation as a writer and his admitted urge to "run, hit, do something with this great amount of muscle frame." The contrast is also reflected in such story titles as "Power and Light: An Idea for Film," a curious parable about women employees of an electric power company who are more powerful and more enlightened than the male characters. In this story, collected in *Captain Maximus,* Polly Buck is a "true warrior for power and light," whereas the men around her are "a blur" (78). She is one of the women in the story who are "doing large things" (84), a fact that pleases a mysterious writer character in the story. Hannah wrote the story as a screenplay and, it seems, also as a free-form exercise in punning on the multiple meanings of "power" and "light."

The confusion that results from this conflict between intellect and violence is seen, for example, in the consternation of the child in *Boomerang* who misinterprets an old man's fear for serenity. Perhaps the child's mistake hints at a more general confusion between traditional and contemporary male role expectations. One of the most articulate expressions of this masculine "dis-ease" is the book *Iron John,* by the poet Robert Bly, who holds

23. Joseph H. Pleck, *The Myth of Masculinity* (Cambridge, Mass., 1981), 140; Mark Gerzon, *A Choice of Heroes: The Changing Faces of American Manhood* (Boston, 1982), 4; Barry Hannah, quoted in R. Vanarsdall, "The Spirits Will Win Through: An Interview with Barry Hannah," *Southern Review,* XIX (1983), 335; William Faulkner, quoted in *A Faulkner Miscellany,* ed. James B. Meriwether (Jackson, Miss., 1973), 158. For recalling this comment of Faulkner's, I am indebted to James Gray Watson, who included it in his paper "William Faulkner: Self-Presentation and Performance," presented at the South Central Modern Language Association conference in San Antonio in 1996.

seminars and retreats to assist men's search for a forgotten heritage of *generative* male power. Bly's theory rests on the psychological truth he finds in the Grimm brothers' "Iron John," the tale of a wild, hairy man at the bottom of a pond, who represents the *"nourishing* dark" part of the male psyche that a boy must have the courage to claim for his own before he can achieve individuation. Bly hastens to add that this "wild man" is not to be confused with the "savage man," who "does great damage to soul, earth, and humankind." Rather, Bly seems to be advocating a masculine counterpart to the feminist movement. In the introduction to *Iron John,* Bly identifies the problem:

> The grief of men has been increasing steadily since the start of the Industrial Revolution and the grief has reached a depth now that cannot be ignored.
>
> The dark side of men is clear. Their mad exploitation of earth resources, devaluation and humiliation of women, and obsession with tribal warfare are undeniable. Genetic inheritance contributes to their obsessions, but also culture and environment. We have defective mythologies that ignore masculine depth of feeling, assign men a place in the sky instead of earth, teach obedience to the wrong powers, work to keep men boys, and entangle both men and women in systems of industrial domination that exclude both matriarchy and patriarchy.[24]

What Bly does not say is that men have contributed to their "defective mythologies" by also assigning women an unrealistic "place in the sky" or else at some opposite extreme, in keeping with the angel/whore myth that dates at least from the Victorian age. The boy books, which came to prominence during the American equivalent of the Victorian era, also reflected failures in culture, including the absence of a male rite of passage and evidence of male "uneasiness with women" that resulted in the attempt to "deny the humiliations of . . . childhood." For example, as Marcia Jacobson points out, Mark Twain felt the need "to go out of his way to mock . . . feminine aspects of his culture" with what amounts to "defensive humor" by creating "sappy women" characters.[25]

This kind of unrealistic expectation about gender roles allows Yelver-

24. Robert Bly, *Iron John: A Book About Men* (Reading, Mass., 1990), x, 6.
25. Jacobson, *Being a Boy Again,* 54–55.

ston, the adult narrator of Hannah's *Boomerang,* to say, "Three months ago
I heard the rumor that women have feelings too" (128). And this defective
mythology is also at work when the same character claims that "women invent the special lovely things of the world" (125) and then implies that his
sexual demands on his wife are incompatible with a woman's nature: "He
knew he was a monster but he had to take her in the mouth this time and
then come on her big generous breasts with the nipples dripping. Why do
men need this? Yelverston asked himself. To make an elegant woman like
her with her dreams of deer submit to this and degrade her?" (126). Had
the passage ended at this point, the lament would have revealed merely the
stale Victorian dichotomy in Yelverston's psyche; but the scene continues
with the wife's positive response to the sexual experience: "He thanked her.
No, she said, thank you, darling. I've never done this for any other man, she
said." And following this, actual closure is achieved when Yelverston "was
so amazed he slept" (126). This remarkable exchange complicates the preceding passage in two ways: Yelverston's account of his wife's answer may be
read as a lie, as wishful thinking, in the adolescent mode reminiscent of
Harry Monroe in *Geronimo Rex,* that she enjoyed the experience; or, suggesting the more contemporary dilemma, it may be taken at face value, in
which case the evidence of equal male and female sexual desire and pleasure
elicits the male's amazement and his consequent withdrawal in sleep.

A related scene in *Geronimo Rex* indicates unabashed adolescent male
amazement at overt female interest in sex—when Harry Monroe and Patsy
Boone make a date to satisfy their mutual curiosity. Harry describes Patsy,
whom he met as they both rehearsed with the Jackson Symphony, as "a
freshman at Millsaps College, and she was nobody's beauty—after the
popping blue eyes and the nice teeth, just a piece of skirt, it seemed" (196).
She has shocked him by making the first move and then, when he enters her
apartment, by tossing her robe aside and "nude, hurling herself on the bed"
(203). Still, as he undresses and toys with the pistol she keeps on her dresser,
he thinks only of the "feast of sight" he himself will make. "I'd done some
push-ups every other week, and knew there were some muscles apparent on
me," he says, and continues, shifting to the present tense, as if narrating a
scene in a movie: "I turn, blinded to her by the effect of my own body. Look
what you are getting for free, Patsy." But when her response to his body is
horror because "men are so ugly," he quickly retreats by climbing out of the
window, only then actually looking at her and noticing that she is lovely.

"My word," he thinks. "I wanted another chance at that, but I was one leg out of the window already. I fell out, on the nasty stems of a hedge. Oh, let me back, but I was too much a fool to climb back up" (204). Harry has thought of girls only as "roaches" and of himself as "Romeo of the Roaches" (200); like the older Yelverston in *Boomerang,* he has thought only of himself, not of the girl, as a true sexual being, one who is capable of sexually aggressive behavior. Even in his quick reevaluation, however, what Harry wants is "another chance at *that*" (emphasis added). The impersonal pronoun points to Hannah's pun on the girl's name, revealing Harry's automatic depersonalization of Patsy. She is a "patsy," a sucker to be victimized, a "piece of skirt," an object that should be his for the taking.

The long history of men burdened with this received unwisdom about women apparently contributes to the adolescent sexual dis-ease—the Albatross about the adult male neck—that in the 1980s and 1990s haunts the sensitive man of "grief," as Bly describes him, prompting him to tell again and again the story of his guilt. Two such guilty tellers are the dual protagonists of Hannah's *Hey Jack!:* Homer, the narrator, and Jack, the coffee-shop owner, the latter of whom "sits with the old fellows around the courthouse, those ancient mariners in this landlocked and soily town" (*HJ,* 6). Homer, named for the ancient Greek quintessential teller of tales, is afflicted with an existential dilemma related not only to Coleridge's Ancient Mariner but also to the psychological agony that has inspired religious confessionals from St. Augustine to Thomas Merton to the modern secular confessional novels of Saul Bellow. A casual reader of Hannah's wild scenarios, told in outrageous, often profane, and sometimes scatological language, might smile at the mention of the confessional, especially the religious confessional. Yet reviewers have linked his name with that of Bellow, and readers familiar with Hannah will have discerned the subtext of religious concern that permeates his fiction. For example, in his review of *Geronimo Rex,* Updike says that Hannah has "the verve of the young Bellow." Donald R. Noble makes a more oblique connection when he notes that Hannah's nomination for the National Book Award for *Geronimo Rex,* in 1972, and the "commercial and . . . critical triumph" of *Ray,* in 1980, led to *Ray's* "taking its place among such novels as Saul Bellow's *Seize the Day* in the Penguin Contemporary American Fiction series." None, however, has explored Hannah's apparent connection with the diarists and novelists who were conducting what Peter M. Axthelm calls a search of their own lives and thoughts for "some form of perception," and who were, as Axthelm says of Bellow's Herzog, "groping for meaning." Such men may suffer from the same syndrome in contemporary society that Gerzon would remedy by what he defines as "true heroism: the courage to explore oneself deeply and to act with self-awareness."[26]

Hannah's obliquely expressed concern with religious faith is apparent, for example, when the narrator in "Love Too Long," from *Airships,* rages at Jesus: "You great bastard! . . . I believed in You on and off all my life!" (15). The cry voices a frustration (at Jesus' failure to set Harry's personal world right) that recalls St. Augustine's prayer: "I was tossed and spilled, floundering in the broiling sea of my fornication, and you said no word." As a confessional medium, however, these stories fit less well in the religious tradition of Augustine and Merton than in the secular tradition of Rousseau, because while searching for absolute meanings, Hannah's protagonists exhibit not so much a need for religious absolution as a fear of shame; thus, their search produces what Peter Brooks cites in Rousseau as "both lies and confessions." Just as fear of judgment by the outside world seemed to "motivate both bad behavior and the confessions that such behavior necessitates" for Rousseau, so it does with Hannah's characters, who well know that "shame happens" (*B,* 92). In his analysis of Book Two of Rousseau's *Confessions,* Brooks employs a method he calls "reading for the plot," perceiving in the movement of the plot a means whereby author, hero, and reader seek "some simulacrum of understanding of how meaning can be construed over and through time." The method works well with Hannah's stories, many of which are structured around a lie/confession trope.[27]

Often, the confessional nature of a story becomes clear through the application of a reader-response technique based on discourse analysis. "Coming Close to Donna" contains another depiction of a male adolescent made to feel sexually inadequate by an aggressive female. By comparing the point of true closure with the possible points in the plot at which Hannah could have ended the story, one can intuit not only the story's meaning but even its genre. Donna has been sexually aroused by the bloody fight in a

26. Updike, "From Dyna Domes to Turkey-Pressing," 124; Donald R. Noble, " 'Tragic and Meaningful to an Insane Degree': Barry Hannah," *Southern Literary Journal,* XV (1982), 36; Peter M. Axthelm, *The Modern Confessional Novel* (New Haven, 1967), 8; Gerzon, *A Choice of Heroes,* 6.

27. St. Augustine, quoted in Axthelm, *The Modern Confessional Novel,* 3; Brooks, *Reading for the Plot,* 31, 35.

cemetery that has resulted in the deaths of two of her suitors, a plot that constitutes a macabre parody of the classic love/death theme. When the teen-aged narrator, who has also witnessed the carnage, is seduced on the spot by the naked Donna, he admits that he gamely "flung in and tried" (*A,* 47). Had the narrative concluded at that point, the story would have been a contemporary example of the comic Gothic grotesque. If a reader perceives a possible closure at that point, he or she may see only the parody of the Gothic, which here approximates slapstick, and may then misapprehend the significance of the rest of the narrative. Current narrative theory suggests, however, that such a response will perhaps say more about the reader's reading experience than about the text. Genre theorist Susan Lohafer explains that when the "macrostructure" of the text reveals a textual grammar or story pattern of comic grotesque incident followed by narrative deflation, then the perceived preclosure point of comedy only serves to signal the true closure of confessional pathos that follows. Thus, if the story had ended when the narrator of "Coming Close to Donna" thinks, "If I were a father, I couldn't conceive of this from my daughter" (46), it would have deflated and upstaged the comic grotesque. The narrator voices something of the same anguish one hears in *The Seven Storey Mountain,* when Trappist monk Thomas Merton says, "I was . . . the prisoner of my own violence and my own selfishness, in the image of the world into which I was born. That world was a picture of Hell, full of men like myself . . . living in fear and hopeless self-contradictory hungers." But Hannah revises even this recognized story grammar by placing the deflation at the midpoint and actually closing with the narrator's return to the scene a year later, when he kills Donna with a tombstone and prepares to get on with his life. He rationalizes, "Some of us are made to live for a long time. Others for a short time. Donna wanted what she wanted. I gave it to her" (47–48). Thus, the plot structure constantly frustrates reader expectations as it veers from Gothic grotesque to confessional pathos to some hybrid mix of existentialism and naturalism that has the effect of poetic justice. Had the incident in "Coming Close to Donna" been an isolated one, it would not exert the tropic force it assumes for a reader who also knows the profusion of such textual grammars in Hannah's fiction.[28]

Plot structures with generic and mood shifts like that in "Coming Close

---

28. Susan Lohafer, "Preclosure and Story Processing," in *Short Story Theory at a Crossroads,* ed. Lohafer and Clarey, 259, 263; Thomas Merton, *The Seven Storey Mountain* (New York, 1962), 9.

to Donna" counter a reader's expectations about meaning. Although Hannah's prose has much in common with the American romance, including passages of poetic lyricism, it does not share Romantic literature's dependence on the paradigmatic exigencies of such lyric modes, which depend on what Peter Brooks calls an "ideal of simultaneity of meaning." Hannah's fiction exhibits, rather, a more syntagmatic dependence on narrative acts that take shape in time, with, to use Brooks's terms, "meanings delayed, partially filled in, stretched out." In these stories, delayed meanings depend on the dream (which is itself a lie), which begets outrageous behavior, which begets more lies, which beget confessions (which may also be lies); the entire sequence debunks the ideal of coherent form and content that characterizes the modern epiphanic short story.[29]

An extended use of the lie/confession trope is found in the story of Alice Lipsey, the beloved daughter of the title character in *Hey Jack!,* whose tawdry affair with rock star Ronnie Foot causes Jack such patriarchal pain. Jack's wish for the innocence of his forty-year-old daughter has been flouted by Foot, who, Jack insists on thinking, "had her" (58). Homer promises to talk to Alice, but instead of an undone spinster he finds a highly sexed woman with "merciless bright eyes" who rides a Harley motorcycle "with no helmet, hair streaming" (71). When he also finds her a complex woman "concerned . . . about Jack's being concerned" but also sexually "voracious," Homer cannot resist her (73–74). Jack eagerly believes the lie of omission in Homer's report on Alice: "She is in no way cheap or cheapened. . . . She's still a queen, your daughter. A very strong woman. I like her laugh. She could . . . eat up all the tawdry measures of Foot without tasting a damned thing." Homer's "wife-to-be," on the other hand, seems instantly aware of his unfaithfulness with Alice, as if he were "a blank sheet of paper on which is written *fornication*" (74).[30] Homer's expounding at length about his own culpability underscores the fact that Hannah's narrator speaks a central concern of the novel: "The heartfelt moans of hypocrisy shook me. What an inadvertent lecher I was, what a dog; I could not bear my transparency and my red lying face. . . . I could not breathe the kind air I used to breathe. I felt to be a new alien to my town, and my sin ran around my legs like dog dyed red" (75). The language of the passage, especially the ludicrous image

---

29. Brooks, *Reading for the Plot,* 20–21.

30. Hereafter, unless otherwise indicated, italics in quoted passages from Hannah's works are in the original text.

of sin as a red dog running around Homer's legs, places both speaker and reader in the gap between religious confession and comedy. One rightly thinks that Homer protests too much. Nevertheless, his self-contradictory effusions recur periodically until true closure is achieved in a tone far removed from the comic grotesque that characterizes several possible preclosure points in the story.

When at the end of the novel Foot has shot Alice and Homer has come to console Jack, Homer reads a passage of military history that is an oblique but not incidental commentary on the tensions between the men. The passage Homer has chosen tells the story of two unequal forces, the U.S. Eighth Army and the Chinese Communists in North Korea, one of which "hadn't read the tragedy that would soon be enacted, [while] the other had written it" (129). General Douglas MacArthur, who had presided at the unconditional surrender of Japan in World War II, had been accustomed to the profession of arms as it had been understood in the United States before the Korean conflict; that is to say, in his experience, American fighting forces conducted war with the aim of unconditional victory. In Korea, however, MacArthur had been charged by the U.S. government to conduct a limited military engagement with an enemy who "had written the book" on that mode of warfare. Ironically, this celebrated general experienced bitter failure at the end of the war, having been fired by President Truman for attempting to widen the scope of the war, never having understood the nature of the enemy (never having "read the tragedy").

At Alice's funeral, Homer is reading "a book about the Eighth Army in Korea" (128), in particular the story of a soldier who remembers "the agony of meeting each incoming little group of survivors and learning who wouldn't be coming back . . . [and of] beating the frozen ground with a stick . . . and wanting to cry for Rex Gunnell and not being able to" (130). Amid this collage of memories about what a "real" man can and cannot do in the face of death, Homer bears witness to the violence of the unequal forces in his own psyche and to the crisis of meaning he suffers when he says all that he can say to mourn Alice:

> I live to say this. Jack lives.
> Alice doesn't.
> Oh, Alice. Hubba hubba, girl. After making it back from the Chinese and with my Silver Star all dogged away behind me, after having that night

of you, and then yourself, a ghost talking to me, and then the last phone call,
and then you dead.
    Killed by a simple stupid millionaire rock star.
    I was pulling my trigger finger in the air again. (131)

Homer lacks the emotional resources to mourn properly, just as he, a Silver Star recipient, has ironically lacked the courage to be truthful about his
and Alice's sexual encounter. Even the combined power of his true feelings
and his innate moral sense is unequal to the forces of latent and unfocused
violence in his culture-conditioned psyche, which has led him to conflate
sex and war and to respond to loss in either arena by "pulling [his] trigger
finger in the air again." Moreover, the psychological realism of Homer's re-
ply is remarkable, for as a veteran of military combat, he responds to great
loss with a blunt recitation of facts that recalls the reactions of actual soldiers in many wars: "I live to say this. Jack lives. Alice doesn't." The Civil
War veteran Captain Praxiteles Swan tells this story: "We all went up to
Gettysburg, the summer of '63: and some of us came back from there; and
that's all except the details." Michael Herr, a former war correspondent, re-
counts a Vietnam soldier's story: "Patrol went up the mountain. One man
came back. He died before he could tell us what happened." Asked for the
rest of the story, the man "just looked like he felt sorry for me," writes Herr,
who calls the story as "one-pointed and resonant as any war story I ever
heard [and further says], it took me a year to understand it."[31]
    The principle of narrative recalcitrance that operates in these war stories
is perhaps most eloquently expressed in Hemingway's novel of World War
I, *A Farewell to Arms,* in which Lieutenant Frederic Henry objects to emo-
tionally patriotic descriptions of war: "There were many words that you
could not stand to hear and finally only the names of places had dignity.
Certain numbers were the same way and certain dates and these with the
names of the places were all you could say and have them mean anything.
Abstract words such as glory, honor, courage, or hallow were obscene beside

    31. Praxiteles Swan, quoted in William Broyles, Jr., *Brothers in Arms* (New York, 1986),
195–96. For this reference I am indebted to Colonel Joseph Cox, U.S. Military Academy,
West Point, N.Y., whose paper " 'Versifying in Earnest': Richard Wilbur's War and His Poetry," was presented at the American Literature Association conference, Baltimore, May 24,
1997. Michael Herr, *Dispatches* (1977; rpr. New York, 1991), 6.

the concrete names of villages, the numbers of roads, the names of rivers, the numbers of regiments and the dates." In *Hey Jack!*, then, Homer's awkward, inarticulate expression of grief is of a piece with historic and literary responses to war and death. His "digression" into military history is not irrelevant in the telling of a story involving death and grief but rather is coherent in terms of his character; it is also coherent in terms of the narrative structure of parody, since it completes an exuberance-to-deflation curve in the plot that inverts and thus parodies the move from devastation to elevation that Joyce Carol Oates has identified in classic tragedy.[32]

Whereas Augustine and Merton find religious answers to their existential plight, Hannah's narrators do not; hence the dilemma that provides the motivation for story after story in which a male protagonist agonizes over the very lusts and violent behaviors in which he engages with such energy and bleak hilarity. But although the fragmented surfaces of Hannah's narratives mirror a world in which meaning has disintegrated into Merton's "picture of Hell, full of men . . . living in fear and hopeless self-contradictory hungers," that these narratives exist—that the narrators keep on talking, and writers keep on writing—is a hopeful sign, as Hannah means it to be, a sign like what Axthelm has described in Bellow as "a means of rebuilding that world around a clearly perceived sense of the self."[33]

In high school, the only building blocks of that self perceived by the adolescent narrator of *Boomerang* are "the horn and my aloofness from the others" (84); he essentially grows up without an enabling male mentor, other than his music teacher, Dick Prenshaw, the character given the actual name of Hannah's high school band director. The obvious affection that Harry, the Barry Hannah character in the novel, exhibits for this teacher no doubt reveals the author's affection for the real Dick Prenshaw. Nevertheless, Harry Monroe credits women as the major influences in his choice of a nonaggressive (literary) career. The narrating persona in *Boomerang* recalls that "it was the women who put up for me when everybody else was saying get ready to be a Real Guy and make a living by being the same old things we are" (92). In terms of Hannah's own literary influences, he told

32. Ernest Hemingway, *A Farewell to Arms* (1929; rpr. New York, 1957), 177–78; Oates, *The Edge of Impossibility*, 4.
33. Axthelm, *The Modern Confessional Novel*, 179.

John Griffin Jones that he reads Eudora Welty "very thoroughly" and believes that Welty's and Faulkner's short stories "had a lot to do with the way I shape them." Robert Bly laments the debilitating results of the adolescent male's having to achieve selfhood without being initiated by an entire community of older male mentors; this custom, long practiced in many societies, has been discarded in the United States. The mentorship of women, of course, is off the scale in the traditional male initiation scheme, although Hannah recognizes several women teachers as instrumental in his decision to be a writer. Bly argues that the lack of a ritual masculine initiation inflicts wounds that contemporary males find almost impossible to heal, a theory that Hannah's fiction seems to bear out in its depiction of young males who suffer from hero-worship and who look for larger-than-life mentors, especially for those who model the culture's prevailing mythos of the sports or military hero.[34]

Hannah's most extensive use of the heroic is seen in his references to war, particularly in (often conflated) fantasies on the Civil War and Vietnam. They are fantasies not only because, as Terrence Rafferty has said of *Airships*, they are the result of "an almost mystical belief in [the] manipulation of language—as if the exact combination of words and images will induce visions, like a prayer," but also because Hannah is not a war veteran. His Ancient Mariner–like compulsion to tell of heroic exploits results in the several voices that tell tales that are sometimes based on the Vietnam experiences of his friend John Quisenberry, a former U.S. Navy pilot, who is another of Hannah's nonfictional characters identified sometimes by fictional names ("Ard Quadberry" in *Airships*) and sometimes by his real name. In the interview with Hannah, when Jones mentioned veterans who have been unable to write about their experiences in Vietnam, Hannah named Quisenberry as being "the same way." "See," Hannah continued, "Quisenberry . . . admires me for writing about the things he went through, being able to, and I admire him for going through them. . . . So it's not like I was showing off like I was an ex-jet pilot." Neither is Hannah simply performing a journalistic service for an actual veteran. His stories are more general inquiries into what it is like to be a hero or, rather, about how far a man will go to satisfy the fantasy of his culture about manly behavior. So-

34. Hannah, quoted in Jones, "Barry Hannah," 141; Bly, *Iron John,* 14–16.

cial psychologist Roger William Brown affirms that in the United States, just as "a *real* boy climbs trees, disdains girls, dirties his knees, [and] plays with soldiers . . . [he] matures into a 'man's man' who plays poker, goes hunting, drinks brandy, and dies in the war." Hannah's stories show the gap between that fantasy and the reality of the hero (and of the lover), and they explore the plight of the American male who must initiate himself into whatever maturity he can manage in life's existential abyss.[35]

Thus, when reviewers like Rafferty complain about Hannah's "burying little references, like land mines, beneath the surface of the story, [so that] we don't trust the terrain enough to see it whole," perhaps they do not realize that these stories bear witness to the truth that there are lies "like land mines, beneath the surface" of all the dreams that boys and young men have grown up with in this country. In "Idaho," from *Captain Maximus*, the narrator's lies about having been in Idaho, when he has only "bought an Idaho patch for [his] jacket" (19), and about having a gun, when he has "only a pencil" in his hand (23), taken together with other references to Ernest Hemingway and the poet Richard Hugo, point to the underlying theme of the lie, which connects the works of these literary heroes of Hannah, who are themselves ambiguously identified with violence and writing, including literary deviousness (the "lie" of literature). Hannah, in a spare style reminiscent of Hemingway's "iceberg" principle, is dealing in "Idaho" with a truth that is too harsh to look at directly: the truth that one lives by lies, including poetic indirection, or what Vanarsdall calls fiction's "sheer lies," which project the illusion of direct confrontation with truth.[36]

Evidence of Hannah's preoccupation with the human propensity for lying is found not only in plots and in titles like "Water Liars" but also in his comments outside of his fiction. His literary depiction of violence—whether on the tennis court, on the football field, or in war—he attributes to a fictional necessity to deal with the lie. Violence, Hannah says, "puts

35. Terrence Rafferty, "Gunsmoke and Voodoo," *Nation*, June 1, 1985, p. 677. Jack Beatty, in his review of *The Tennis Handsome, New Republic*, April 18, 1983, p. 39, calls Hannah's Quisenberry character "the obligatory Vietnam veteran [as a] stock symbol of rage and anomie." Jones, "Barry Hannah," 150; Roger William Brown, *Social Psychology* (New York, 1965), 161, emphasis Brown's.

36. Rafferty, "Gunsmoke and Voodoo," 677; Vanarsdall, "The Spirits Will Win Through," 319.

your back up against the wall. People tend to lie less in conditions of violent behavior . . . there is something direct and honest about [such violence]," he told McCaffery and Gregory. Thus, Hannah's fiction is more than a tour de force of language, as some have called it. It is, rather, part confessional ode and part celebration of his attempt to put a lying culture's "back up against the wall" and to "make something happen in vacant air [that is] a sweet revenge" on "the whole lying opera" of cultural memory that constitutes the American dream, to rage against the painfully slow dying of the defective mythologies that keep men boys. Although, as Allen Shepherd has pointed out, Hannah's plots are not conventional, they cohere in what constitutes a significant postmodern "chaos" of miniplots designed to appeal to the narrative desires of writer, would-be fictional hero, and reader, to find meaning in the gaps between dreams, lies, and confessions. They also cohere in their use of a salient feature of the boy book subgenre: the writer's re-creation of his childhood self as a clue to his adult identity.[37]

37. McCaffery and Gregory, "An Interview with Barry Hannah," in *Alive and Writing,* ed. McCaffery and Gregory, 120–21; Allen Shepherd, " 'Something Wonderful to Tell': Barry Hannah's *Boomerang," Southern Review,* XIX (1983), 73.

· Two ·

Battles for Identity:
Debunking the Unitary Self and Story

When I talk to my son, Ross thought, it is comfortable for both of us
to pretend that I am a hack and he the flaming original; it gives us defined places for discussion.
—Barry Hannah, "Hey, Have You Got a Cig,
the Time, the News, My Face?"

A STABLE SENSE of identity has been an elusive goal for southerners since
antebellum times, primarily because of the complex and powerful forces
brought to bear on the individual psyches of men and women—black and
white—by two traumatic facts of history. The first was their mutual bondage to chattel slavery, the South's "peculiar institution" that had seemed so
necessary for the plantation economy. Lillian Smith, in her memoir *Killers
of the Dream* (1949), argues that the "race-sex-sin spiral . . . [that character-
ized] the white man's roles as slaveholder and Christian and puritan . . . exact[ed] far more than the strength of his mind could sustain," resulting in
a lasting legacy of "guilt, shame, fear, [and] lust" so strong that even children were aware of the close link between race and sex. "Therefore," Smith
recalls, "when we as small children crept over the race line and ate and
played with Negroes or broke other segregation customs known to us, we
felt the same dread fear of consequences, the same overwhelming guilt we

felt when we crept over the sex line and played with our body or thought thoughts about God or our parents that we knew we must not think." The second source of trauma was the Civil War: the South's defeat and surrender in battle, with its legacy of shame mixed, ironically, with nostalgia for an idealized notion of the "lost cause." It is little wonder that this cumulative psychic strain, which C. Vann Woodward calls "the burden of southern history," should be apparent in the imaginative literature written by southerners of the generations following close on the traumatic historical events; but to find, in works written more than one hundred years after the end of the Civil War, similar emotions linked to the same causes suggests more than a literature of memory. The impetus for much literature of the contemporary South seems to be the tension produced by one or more of the following: the continuing power of a cultural mythology that defines expectations of class, race, and gender; pressures of a new moral consciousness; new injuries to old wounds.[1]

If the new moral consciousness engendered by the civil rights and women's movements called attention to the damage wrought by cultural values based on patriarchal and other hegemonic power structures, the Vietnam experience provided many new injuries, both physical and psychological. In a book on storytellers of the Vietnam generation, David Wyatt argues that literary generations are defined by, among other things, "the impact of a traumatic historical incident or episode . . . [which] creates the sense of a rupture in time and gathers those who confront it into a shared sense of ordeal." Whether they, their friends, or someone in their families were the actual combatants, the writers born between 1940 and 1950 are those most directly influenced by the Vietnam period, from the committal of U.S. troops to Vietnam in 1965 to troop withdrawal in 1973. Recalling the comments of individual writers about their frustration with impersonal accounts of the history of the Vietnam era, Wyatt focuses on the idea of story as a formal structure that mediates between the public history and the intensely personal individual responses to the chaos of this "rupture in time." Historically, the concept of story is more than that of mediator; it has been understood as a force for coherence, a form imposed upon the

---

1. Lillian Smith, *Killers of the Dream* (Rev. ed., 1961; rpr. New York, 1994), 120–21; C. Vann Woodward, *The Burden of Southern History* (Rev. ed.; Baton Rouge, 1968).

chaos of experience. Philip D. Beidler points out that the best writers about Vietnam are not only committed to the concrete reporting of the experience as one that "actually seizes upon us . . . as a thing of the senses, of the emotions, of the intellect, of the spirit"; they are also involved in "a primary process of sensemaking, of discovering the peculiar ways in which the experience of the war can now be made to signify within the larger evolution of culture as a whole," contributing to "the process of cultural myth-making" and to experiences common to all people. Wyatt believes that the so-called Vietnam generation desperately desires its stories to be this kind of formative force. Comparing it with Eliotic "fragments shored against ruins," he argues that story, as that formative force, is the means by which those who write about Vietnam "resist the dominant and violently inarticulate contemporary discourse." But many tellers of war stories seem to think of their narratives not as "formative" forces but rather as extreme versions of that discourse's violence and inarticulateness. In *The Things They Carried,* Tim O'Brien points out that "a true war story" does not "generalize"; and he suggests that such stories fail to cohere in the kind of formal unity that lends itself to the establishing of a theme that can be recognized by either author or reader. "Often," O'Brien says, "in a war story there is not even a point, or else the point doesn't hit you until twenty years later in your sleep." Moreover, he asserts that "you can tell a true war story by the way it never seems to end. Not then, not ever. . . . All you can do is tell it one more time, patiently, adding and subtracting, making up a few things to get at the real truth. . . . And in the end, of course, a true war story is never about war. It's about sunlight. It's about the special way that dawn spreads out on a river when you know you must cross the river and march into the mountains and do things you are afraid to do. It's about love and memory. It's about sorrow. It's about sisters who never write back and people who never listen."[2]

Central to Barry Hannah's narrative structures is the chaos of war, both *as war* and as metaphor for the more general violence and inarticulateness of his generation. His fiction is intensely concerned with the kind of shattered individual psyches that Michael Herr, in writing about Vietnam, rec-

2. David Wyatt, *Out of the Sixties: Storytelling and the Vietnam Generation* (New York, 1993), 2–7; Philip D. Beidler, *American Literature and the Experience of Vietnam* (Athens, Ga., 1982), xiii; Tim O'Brien, *The Things They Carried* (Boston, 1990), 83, 88, 91.

ognized by battle-fatigued soldiers' "eyes that poured out a steady charge of wasted horror." As such, Hannah's stories show how the habit of violence is both cause and consequence of the divided self, for the fragmented narrative of a Hannah war story accurately reflects the lives of its characters. Mark Charney argues that these stories satirize the characters' "inability to make sense out of life"; yet for Hannah, as well as for his fictional narrators, each story constitutes an attempt at making sense, such as Beidler finds in other Vietnam literature.[3]

In contrast to other writers, Hannah does not depict Vietnam as a unique experience, as does Philip Caputo, who calls it "the only . . . [war] we have ever lost." Rather, Hannah's fiction presents Vietnam in the context of the history of the South and its lost cause in the Civil War: as a contemporary manifestation of southern traditions of violence, honor, and dishonor. His approach is appreciated by Owen Gilman, Jr., whose chapter on Hannah's literary use of the theme Richard Slotkin identified in American history and culture as "regeneration through violence" is the most significant study to date on Hannah. Gilman shows the extent to which in many southern writers, and in the southern imagination in general, Vietnam was "prefigured in the history of the South." To Hannah's characters, it is one of two "unfinished" wars, in the sense of unresolved issues that continue to exert force over their lives.[4]

Hannah's unstable male narrators refight the same wars by retelling the same stories, as if the next telling might provide meaning, perhaps vindication, or at least closure. They long for the good fight, even the good death, which is necessary to a culturally enforced idea of honor but which is continually undermined by the perverse human inability to avoid dishonorable acts. His fragmented, often surreal, narratives are at once postmodern and squarely in the mainstream of the American short story tradition, which includes both the epiphanic story of innocence, experience, and integration and its complement, the nonepiphanic story, described by Leitch

3. Herr, *Dispatches,* 22; Mark Charney, *Barry Hannah* (New York, 1991), 64.
4. Philip Caputo, *A Rumor of War* (1977; rpr. New York, 1994), xii; Owen W. Gilman, Jr., "Regenerative Violence; or, Grab Your Saber, Ray," in Gilman, *Vietnam and the Southern Imagination* (Jackson, Miss., 1992), esp. p. 87; Richard Slotkin, *Regeneration Through Violence: The Mythology of the American Frontier, 1600–1860* (Middletown, Conn., 1973).

as a means to "the author's unmaking and the audience's unknowing." Hannah most often writes the latter, the kind of story that exhibits what Leitch calls a "debunking rhythm" in which antithesis is unresolved; epiphany is not achieved. Such a narrative rhythm, Leitch says, is integral to the thematic debunking of "the concept of a public identity, a self that acts in such a knowable, deliberate way as to assert a stable, discrete identity . . . that was only an illusion to begin with." Vietnam is a subject made for such a technique, since that experience forced the entire nation to rethink the contradictory nature of its self-concept and its public identity. It is also a subject that embodies the paradox of story fragments that try but always fail to shore up the ragged holes in individual psyches as well as in cultural myths of heroism.[5]

Hannah did not serve in Vietnam, but he was twenty-three when the American involvement there began in 1965; in published interviews and in novels and short stories he bears witness to his belonging to the Vietnam generation. Hannah's interest in military history, Vietnam, and war in general is no doubt complemented by his admiration for the fiction of two other famous American noncombatants, Hemingway and Faulkner, with whose work his own has a complex relation. And since Hannah is a southerner, his concept of war is always colored by the peculiar traditions of violence and the codes of honor, military and otherwise, that coexist in the southern mind. If Hannah's fiction is not the direct response of a veteran, it is, nevertheless, a response that resonates with the knowledge of wars and other national traumas. Asked about Vietnam, Hannah recalled, "You woke up every day with that war on your TV. . . . You were watching 'The Three Stooges' or whatever, and the next thing on was bloody corpses and body counts [and] the copters always." Asked about a locus of violence closer to home, the civil rights movement in Mississippi, Hannah replied, "You could get a pistol pulled on you for wearing tennis shoes at one point . . . [because it] meant 'hippies,' 'Freedom Riders.'"[6]

The other war that most directly informs Hannah's fiction, the Civil War, or as many southerners prefer, the War Between the States, does so in

5. Leitch, "The Debunking Rhythm of the American Short Story," in *Short Story Theory at a Crossroads,* ed. Lohafer and Clarey, 131–46.

6. Hannah, quoted in Jones, "Barry Hannah," 145, 150.

part because of his having grown up surrounded by memorials of the South's honored dead. Allen Tate, in "Ode to the Confederate Dead," asks what is to be done with such memories:

> What shall we say who have knowledge
> Carried to the heart? Shall we take the act
> To the grave? Shall we, more hopeful, set up the grave
> In the house? The ravenous grave?

Historically, that is exactly what southerners have done. In Hannah's words, "Growing up here, you can almost feel Vicksburg if you're alive. . . . You grow up in that park with those gloomy old busts and those cannons. It's easy to be full of history. . . . You know things just by growing up, like [the fact that] Jackson was Chimneyville." Hannah has the southerner's comprehension of the qualities basic to southern life in general and to war in particular: honor and its mirror image, shame. According to historian Bertram Wyatt-Brown, honor and shame "cannot be understood apart from . . . [each] other. [A southerner] was expected to have a healthy sense of shame, that is, a sense of his own honor. Shamelessness signified a disregard for both honor and disgrace. When shame was imposed by others, honor was stripped away."[7]

Hannah's protagonists are driven by inherited ideas about honor, shame, and vengeance—from ancient Indo-European tribal concepts to Old Testament imperatives—and by the American, especially southern, translation of these ideas into a personal code that assumes the public nature of private acts. The South has understood the primal honor code as one "designed to give structure to life and meaning to valor, hierarchy, and family protection," says Wyatt-Brown, "but its almost childlike clarity, its seeming innocence, contained inner contradictions. Within the ethic, there was a conflict never wholly mastered, a point at which the resolutions and the alternations of the system broke down . . . [because of] the discrepancy between honor as obedience to superior rank and the contrary duty to achieve place for oneself and family." Although meant to "prevent unjustified vio-

---

7. *Ibid.,* 147–48; Bertram Wyatt-Brown, *Honor and Violence in the Old South* (New York, 1986), viii.

lence, unpredictability, and anarchy," the honor code could lead to "that very nightmare."[8]

In Hannah's fiction, the individual continues to do battle with the code by both aspiring to and struggling against its mythic, heroic ideal; conflicts between the exigencies of that public ideal and those of the private self are at the heart of the psychic ruptures in his characters. In their search for honor, love, and power, they tell lies, act reprehensibly, and are in general at the mercy of their self-defeating behavior. All the heroes of Hannah's stories imagine "high and valiant stuff," as does Horace in "Scandal d'Estime," a story from *Bats Out of Hell* (217); but when they cannot live up to such ideals, they resort to dreams, lies, and confessions about them. Reflecting this disjunction, the stories themselves are ruptured by unsettling shifts, gaps, and disavowals of their own truth. Describing such disunities in Vietnam literature, Beidler notes that "everything from official euphemism to battlefield slang seem[s] the product of some insane genius for making reality and unreality—and thus, by implication, sense and nonsense—as indistinguishable as possible."[9]

The trauma of war erupts in Hannah's stories, even amid peacetime settings, through the violent and bizarre words, thoughts, and acts of his characters, one of whom is modeled on John Quisenberry. In "Testimony of Pilot," set in Hannah's hometown of Clinton, Mississippi, Arden Quadberry is "a genius" at playing the saxophone in high school (*A*, 25) who becomes "the genius master of his dragon," according to William Howly, the autobiographical narrator in the story (39). Before he leaves for Vietnam to fly F-8s off an aircraft carrier, to escort B-52s into Vietnam, Quadberry puts his jet down at the airport in Jackson, Mississippi, to tell his girlfriend goodbye. However, he not only refuses to disembark but refuses to kiss Lilian; he says only one thing: "I am a dragon. America the beautiful, like you will never know." Lilian does not understand, but William knows that Quadberry's purpose has been to identify completely with the airplane. "It wasn't just him he wanted us to see," William tells her. "It was him in that jet he wanted us to see. He *is* that black jet. You can't kiss an airplane" (38).

8. Wyatt-Brown, *Honor and Violence in the Old South*, 25–39.

9. Beidler, *American Literature and the Experience of Vietnam*, 5.

"Testimony of Pilot" follows Quadberry into action, where he demonstrates that "as on saxophone, [he] had endless learned technique. He'd put his jet perpendicular in the air and make the SAMs look silly"; he continues such death-defying stunts until back injuries from two ejections from downed planes render him "out of this war and all wars for good" (40–41). The ironic conclusion has Quadberry scheduled for surgery, which will either cure his back injury or kill him. The surgeon, "some genius from Johns Hopkins Hospital . . . [who is] just his age," and thus a sort of alter ego for Quadberry, "lost him [and] Quadberry died with his Arabian nose up in the air." In the final line, "That is why I told this story and will never tell another," the word "that" refers to the irony of the pilot's death not in heroic battle but during a surgical procedure with a "seventy-five . . . [percent chance to] be successful" (44); in other words, no logic can explain it. The final comment, the extra "note" in the rhythm of the narrative that creates its debunking, connects this story to other Vietnam literature by both structurally and thematically signifying the impossibility of a war story's ability to present a coherent, satisfying epiphany or even a reliable sense of its protagonist's identity. In addition to Arden Quadberry's earlier self-description as "a dragon," an extinct beast-monster, the story itself is the "testimony" of one casualty of Vietnam who "lost his gamble at Emory Hospital in Atlanta" (44). Both his identity as a war hero and that as a "genius" are deflated as they are inexplicably merged with that of his "genius" surgeon; since the autobiographical "I" in the last line obviously will tell other stories, this one ends with a lie that calls the entire "testimony" into question.

In "Midnight and I'm Not Famous Yet," another story from *Airships,* Hannah illustrates the dilemma of honor betrayed into shame. It is the story of two young soldiers from Mississippi who have the apparent good luck to capture the Vietnamese general Li Dap and his gunner, the two occupants of a tank that had foundered in a pond. The general has been educated at the Sorbonne and is a history buff. The narrator, Captain Bobby Smith, learns from his prisoner that Li Dap's downfall is due to his fascination with "Robert Lee and the strategy of Jeb Stuart, whose daring circles around an immense army captured his mind." As Bobby tells the story, "Li Dap had tried to circle left with twenty thousand and got the hell kicked out of him by idle Navy guns sitting outside Gon. He just wasn't very bright. He had half his army climbing around these bluffs, no artillery or air force with them, and it was New Year's Eve for our side" (110–11). Because Li Dap is captured while personally leading this insanely daring attack "as an example to [his] men," Bobby recognizes and honors the heroic ideal the enemy officer represents. In the mind of the young southern captain, the wars and cultures merge; to him, "all this hero needed was a plumed hat" to be seen as an officer of the Confederate States of America (113).

Tubby Wooten, the other American soldier in the story, is a photographer who enjoys a brief reverie of the fame that will surely accrue to him when his prize-winning photographs of the captured general are published in *Time* or *Newsweek*. Almost immediately after Li Dap's capture, however, his unit is attacked by the North Vietnamese army. Tubby is killed, and when a Vietnamese soldier is about to bayonet the American soldier guarding Li Dap, Bobby "burn[s] them all up" with a phosphorus shotgun (116). For killing "a captured general" and allowing "twenty gooks to come up on us like that," he is demoted to lieutenant and sent home, his own dream of honor reversed to shame. "That's all right," he rationalizes. "I've got four hundred and two boys out there—the ones that got back—who love me and know the truth, who love me *because* they know the truth." But the picture of Li Dap haunts him; in Tubby's photograph of him, the Vietnamese general "looked wonderful—strained, abused and wild, his hair flying over his eyes while he's making a statement full of conviction" (117). Thus, through the ironic contrast of a Vietnamese officer who dies Hemingway's "good death" and a southern soldier who not only "is not famous yet" but who dreams of an honor that he turns into shame by his own firepower, Hannah evokes the psychological chaos of war and its literature.

Hannah's narrative method in "Midnight and I'm Not Famous Yet" resembles that of many other writers of Vietnam literature, who have made the modernists' stream-of-consciousness into a postmodernist technique by merging characters' thoughts and dreams so that often neither character nor reader can easily distinguish between past war experiences and present reality. The classic contemporary example is Tim O'Brien's *Going after Cacciato*, in which the fine line between the narrator's imagination and his memory is always in doubt. Private Paul Berlin's tale is anchored so loosely to his guard post on the beach that it seems less real than his picaresque account of an entire company's adventures through and out of Vietnam, across continents, in search of one AWOL soldier. Such a narrative technique seems especially relevant to Vietnam literature, since many veterans of the Vietnam conflict suffer from post-traumatic stress disorder, an affliction so named because of the continuing psychological trauma caused by memories of war so vivid that they may seem more real than a veteran's actual postwar life. As Michael Bibby asserts, "Vietnam is the war . . . that introduced 'post-traumatic stress' into our national lexicon. Indeed the Vietnam War signifies a trauma in American culture, and like victims of trauma, Americans write and rewrite the war in order to be purged of it." The illness' pervasive and continuing power over the lives of veterans and their families is seen not only in clinical practice but also in both fiction and nonfiction, written by both men and women and both veterans and nonveterans.[10]

Among Vietnam fiction written by nonveterans, Bobbie Ann Mason's *In Country* focuses on a young girl's attempt to understand her uncle, a veteran who suffers from the disorder, and her attempt to know something about her father, who was killed in Vietnam before she was born. Perhaps the most compelling fictional depiction of post-traumatic stress disorder written by a Vietnam veteran is Philip Caputo's *Indian Country,* in which the shifting, converging borders of wartime memory and present reality generate extreme mental states in Caputo's protagonist. Robert Olen Butler has also created a soldier-protagonist who merges dreams of his father with dreams and realities of Saigon even before he leaves for home. In the darkness of his "Eden," his and Lanh's room, he thinks it is "filled, with people. No. Just the thoughts of people—all those he'd been close to or had expected to be . . . so that what the room was filled with now was their absence." The Vietnam theme and the merging-of-realities technique common to O'Brien, Mason, Caputo, Butler, Hannah, and others has also been adapted for so-called pop fiction, for example, in the murder mysteries of James Lee Burke. Since one of Burke's protagonists, New Orleans police detective Dave Robicheaux, is a Vietnam veteran, it is perhaps natural for him to relive his Vietnam experiences in what constitutes a subtheme in

10. Tim O'Brien, *Going After Cacciato* (New York, 1978); Michael Bibby, " 'Where Is Vietnam?: Antiwar Poetry and the Canon," *College English,* LV (1993), 159.

this series of novels. However, in the neo-Gothic thriller *In the Electric Mist with Confederate Dead,* Burke gives the Civil War a role similar to that of Vietnam, as the ghost of a Confederate general appears intermittently in the mists of the Vietnam-like Louisiana swamp, helping Robicheaux to solve the murder. Unlike Barry Hannah, Burke does not merge the two wars in his hero's mind; but his use of both the Civil War and Vietnam in dream-vision sequences that interact with more mundane reality suggests that he, like Hannah and others, sees the two wars as mysteriously linked. They seem linked not only in the more theoretical terms of psychological phenomena but also in the more personal terms of heroically idealized memories conditioned by cultural myths. These myths would almost guarantee trauma because of the defeat associated with Vietnam, a condition once unthinkable in this country, except to southerners.[11]

As Tim O'Brien says of all "true war stories," Hannah's "Midnight and I'm Not Famous Yet" may not be about war but "about love and memory." Nevertheless, there is a debunking of the heroic ideal in the story and a concomitant debunking structural rhythm that results from protagonist Bobby Smith's inability to resolve his shame at being demoted in rank, especially in comparison with the heroism of the captive enemy he has killed. There is no moral here, no epiphany, and no resolution. Bobby is even more alienated in the larger civilian society to which he returns, now that he has failed to measure up to the myth of the hero that American culture continues to validate. As Bobby recognizes in the gallery's despair over a favorite golfer who loses a match, the myth reveals itself even in peacetime, in society's worship of the fittest. "Fools! Fools! [he thinks]. Love it! Love the loss as well as the gain. Go home and dig it. Nobody was killed. We saw victory and defeat, and they were both wonderful" (*A,* 118). Yet Bobby's fine-sounding rationale is hollow, since it is belied by his inability to countenance his own loss of stature. His fragile sense of self is apparent in his confession that, back home, he "crawled in bed with almost anything that would have [him]" (117).[12]

Some of Hannah's finest writing about war is included in the collection

11. Bobbie Ann Mason, *In Country* (New York, 1985); Philip Caputo, *Indian Country* (New York, 1987); Robert Olen Butler, *The Alleys of Eden* (New York, 1981), 70; James Lee Burke, *In the Electric Mist with Confederate Dead* (New York, 1993).

12. O'Brien, *The Things They Carried,* 91.

Bats Out of Hell, which takes its title partly from the story "Bats Out of Hell Division." The narrator is a Confederate soldier whose story reflects the realism of the South's defeat—of honor turned to shame for an entire region, and of a betrayal of the soldiers' self-image that involves a falling away of everything they had depended on. About the military action central to the plot, the unnamed narrator relates that "the charge, our old bread and butter, has withered into the final horror of the field, democracy" (44). In other words, the division has lost its coherent structure. Moreover, the beleaguered soldiers, constantly tortured by the smells of cooking food coming from the Union camp, are betrayed by their starved and failing bodies, so "gaunt . . . [and] almost not there" (48) that the enemy bullets haven't much of a target. They are also betrayed by their minds, and even the general is "criminally insane just like the rest of them" (45).

On the level of language, the theme of betrayal is implicit in the many self-contradictions in the narrative. The story begins: "We, in a ragged bold line across their eyes, come on." Here is Hannah's version of many an actual battle in the South's lost cause, wherein honor and glory were earned only by continuing to advance when hope of victory was as ragged as the Confederate soldiers' uniforms. In this war story, ironic reversal is seen in the backward waving of the Confederate colors, which continue to advance while bearer after bearer is shot out from under them. "Shreds of the flag leap back from the pole held by Billy, then Ira," we are told; but fearing shame more than death, the soldiers go forward, while the tattered shreds of flag seem to point to the rear. "We . . . are not getting on too well," admits the chronicler of the Bats Out of Hell Division. "They have shot hell out of us. More properly we are merely the Bats by now. Our cause is leaking, the fragments of it left around those great burned holes, as if their general put his cigar into the document a few times" (43). The story presents a paradigm of the Hannah hero, whose cause is always "leaking" and whose personality, like that of the Confederate chronicler, is defined by "fragments" and "great burned holes," which betray the truth that its "hell-fire" or spirit has been devastated.

The prospect and thus the story would be unbearable were it not for the bleak hilarity and the desperate energy of these would-be heroes. "But we're still out there," the narrator tells us; "We gain by inches, then lose by yards. . . . By now you must know that half our guns are no good, either. . . . Estes—as I spy around—gets on without buttocks, just hewn off one sorry cowardly night. . . . I have become the scribe—not voluntarily, but because all limbs are gone except my writing arm" (43). Note that it is not Estes but rather in Hannah's comic mixture of personification and metonymy, "one sorry . . . night" that is branded as "cowardly." Estes, a true son of the Confederacy, will not shame his comrade by calling *him* cowardly.

The illusion of the heroic also causes the narrator to cling to a shred of vanity about his personal appearance. He sees himself in the image of a southern figural hero, a staple character in southern fiction, described by Michael Kreyling as a nearly perfect physical specimen and one who can "instantly render the provisional nature of any situation into a part of a consecrated pattern." The chief exemplar is General Robert E. Lee, commander of the Confederate forces, whose personal appearance, according to a fellow cadet at West Point, "surpassed in manly beauty any cadet in the corps." Another model is J. E. B. Stuart, who makes cameo appearances in several Hannah stories. Stuart was also a handsome West Pointer who was said to represent "the ideal of Southern manhood." Perhaps aspiring to this ideal (although he is actually a parody of it), Hannah's narrator in "Bats Out of Hell Division" says that his comrades and captain think him "not unsightly" and the unit's "benign crone of a nurse" says he is a "man of some charm."[13]

In a passage that ponders the role of this front-line nurse, the narrator thinks, "Maybe they use her to make us fight for home"; but he immediately contradicts himself: "Better to think she's part of no plan at all. The best things in life, or whatever you call *this*, happen like that. . . . This marks the very thing, most momentous, I am writing about" (43). In this statement, the narrator suggests that chaos—"no plan at all"—is inherent not only in war but in life, and perhaps in the story, too. Moreover, in his analogy of war's death-in-life situation with "the best things in life," accomplished with Candide-like humor and a best-of-all-possible-worlds manner, the narrator articulates and parodies the ironic truth that war holds a fierce attraction for soldiers. In fact, he interrupts his own story to

---

13. Michael Kreyling, *Figures of the Hero in Southern Narrative* (Baton Rouge, 1987), 4, 110; Kenneth Seib, "'Sabers, Gentlemen, Sabers': The J. E. B. Stuart Stories of Barry Hannah," *Mississippi Quarterly*, XLV (1991–92), 42–43.

tell of a soldier killed in the previous Mexican war who "returned out of the
very earth once he heard another cracking good one was on. At last, at last!
The World War of his dreams." In this fantastic story-within-a-story, the
dead-undead soldier rhapsodizes, " 'There *is* a God, and God is *love!* . . .
Brother against brother! In my lifetime! Can Providence be this good?' "
(45). The irony in Hannah's treatment of the romantic mythology of war is
heightened by the counterpoint that occurs when his narrator admits, "I
have license to exaggerate, as I have just done," and then qualifies *that* revision by continuing, without even a pause, "but many would be horrified to
know how little" (45). Such constant self-revision, which is typical of many
fictional and autobiographical war stories, contributes to the debunking
narrative rhythm that Leitch calls "the author's unmaking and the audience's unknowing."

Throughout "Bats Out of Hell Division," the narrative shifts between
the grimly real and the surreal, sometimes approaching the operatic. The
term *operatic,* originally denoting the implausible, artificial, or histrionic
nature of opera, can be extended to describe the exaggerated or heightened
nature of dreams or, in Hannah's fiction, of memories. In "Testimony of Pilot," for example, the narrator laments, "Memory, the whole lying opera of
it, is killing me now" (*A,* 32). This pattern of incongruities in Hannah's
version of the literature of memory conforms to a pattern Beidler has described in many Vietnam narratives, in which Vietnam is at the same time
and "in a single moment, dreadful, funny, nightmarish, ecstatic." In the
midst of this bizarre foreign place, "innocent, bloodied eighteen-year-olds
tossed off smooth, ugly, epigrammatic zingers," Beidler notes, in a passage
that could aptly describe some of Hannah's characters. "Americans in Vietnam looked for something, anything, to sustain the flow of psychic energy
that finally had to substitute for even the most remote sense of purpose,"
Beidler continues; thus, some of the unreal reality of the Vietnam experience is the result of soldiers who were "stoned out of their skulls, weighed
down with their totems, their talismanic nicknames and buddy-lore, their
freaky bravado, Jim Morrison and Janis Joplin and Jimi Hendrix and the
Stones blasting away in their ears."[14]

In Hannah's story, the soldiers of the Bats Out of Hell Division, so

14. Beidler, *American Literature and the Experience of Vietnam,* 12–14.

skinny that the Union bullets cannot hit them, advance through the smoke with "happy bayonets high," when they realize they "are running in sudden silence . . . [because the Union troops] are not firing anymore." Here Hannah debunks the idea of war as glorious when his narrator describes the effect of the doomed Confederates' alleged "happy bayonets" on the Union general, who agonizes over the carnage. Through the haze the southern troops are astonished to see General Kosciusky screaming first at his own troops and then at the Confederates: " 'Stop it! Stop it! I can't take it anymore. The lost cause! Look at you! My holy God, gray brothers, behold yourself! Cease fire! Cease it all!' " Then, contrary to all military logic, Kosciusky surrenders, shouting, "The music. The Tchaikovsky! You wretched specters coming on! It's too much. Too much" (49). At the climax of this fantastic opera, the "stunned" Confederate general takes Kosciusky's sword, while the narrator undercuts his own story by admitting its improbability: "Nothing in history led us to believe we had not simply crossed over to paradise itself and were dead just minutes ago" (49).[15]

As the historian of the Bats Out of Hell Division, the scribe can tell the story any way he wishes, so he gives the Bats the victory and, by extension, implies a dream self that fits the South's ideal of the victorious warrior. Yet the story ends with a mundane anticlimax about what to name the battle, evincing a narrative technique that counters the operatic climax with the matter-of-fact voice of the scribe, who has continually countered his own "license to exaggerate" (45). Each successive narrative act undercuts the previous act; thus the story's structure, instead of providing a more traditional formal coherence, reflects, by its surface incoherence, a narrative consciousness shattered by violent internal and external conflicts. Its non-epiphanic conclusion deflates the heroic rhetoric of war as it debunks the concept of meaningful epiphany.

15. The name bears a close resemblance to that of General Thaddeus Kosciusko, the Polish officer and engineer who designed and built the fortifications at West Point during the Revolutionary War. He also served in the Continental Army as commander of the engineering corps. A statue of Kosciusko on the grounds of the U.S. Military Academy at West Point commemorates his service to this country. His sword, part of the West Point Museum's collection, is inscribed: "Draw me not without reason, Sheathe me not without honor." See Ellen B. Heinback and Gale G. Kohlhagen, *Guide to West Point and the Hudson Valley* (New York, 1990), 33.

The subject of war, so important to many of Hannah's stories, is often related to a character's anxiety over identity. In "Even Greenland," from *Captain Maximus*, two pilots have apparently been involved in a longtime competition of writing and telling each other stories about self-defining experiences going back to their childhood in Mississippi, where it is important to both of them to have been "the first up and there's been nobody in the snow, no footsteps" (32). Even something as extraordinary as snow in Mississippi, if others have seen it, is not "fresh" anymore, because "there were eyes that had used it up some" (32). With their F-14 on fire as they try to land at Miramar Air Base, the narrator urges John to eject, but he will not, because his going down with the plane will outdo the other. As Michael Spikes points out, "The desire to secure a [Harold] Bloom-like poetic identity and the fear of failing are so strong in John that they lead him to commit suicide."[16]

In "Upstairs, Mona Bayed for Dong," the Persian Gulf war serves as a background for meditations about life and death for a middle-aged couple. Narrator Nick Poore describes his wife, Vaughtie, as "pregnant at forty" (*BOH*, 272), obsessed with youth, "frightened being forty" (270), and worried about dying. He reveals himself to be "a brigadier general in the Guard" who has never seen action and who wants to videotape Vaughtie, "right at the beginning of the long downward curve into age" before he leaves for Desert Storm (270). The story contrasts the idea of dying, both literally—in war while he is in the Persian Gulf—and metaphorically—in the illicit relationship Nick has when he returns to San Diego. He was, he says, "dying in this low arrangement with the flutist, while my wife was back at the house preparing life" (276). The fact that his wife is about to give birth seems to make the matter more acute for both of them. Nick, who is a "good soldierly coward . . . plung[es] around trying to find something greatly worthy in [him]self" (278–79) and, finding nothing, decides to assert himself by evicting his sister-in-law and taking a whip to flick a cigarette out of Vaughtie's mouth. Ironically, the combination of his new attitude and her giving birth seems to generate new identities in himself and Vaughtie: she becomes aggressive and begins going into the basement,

16. Michael P. Spikes, "Barry Hannah in the American Grain," *Notes on Mississippi Writers*, XXIII (1991), 30.

where she practices "cracking the whip . . . [while he is] holding the baby" (281), in a gender role reversal reminiscent of that in Bobbie Ann Mason's "Shiloh." Mason's story ends with an apparently failed marriage; Hannah's ends as Vaughtie orders, " 'Husband. Come down here, would you? Bring your cigarette.' "[17]

The title of "Hey, Have You Got a Cig, the Time, the News, My Face?" obliquely announces its theme as the search for identity. In this story, E. Dan Ross is worried about his son Newt, a poet with a drinking problem who has been fired "in scandal from a bad school" (*BOH,* 306) and who has, Dan thinks unfortunately, married Ivy Pilgrim: "The marriage should not have taken place. Newt was unable to swim rightly in his life and times. The girl was not pregnant, neither was she rich. . . . He could imagine a hypersensitive dirt-town twit leeching onto his boy" (305). Dan, a biographer himself, declares that "Newt must prevail, have a 'story' " (306). Like many of Hannah's stories, this one is concerned with the act of writing. Dan Ross speculates about biography that "there was always a great lie in supposing any life was significant at all . . . [and that] some were simply addicted to writing, victims of inner logorrhea . . . [who had] no lives at all . . . [because] they simply could not stop observing, never seeing much, really" (311). As in other stories, Hannah's watching protagonist imagines himself "in a delicious advantage . . . [to] shoot some innocent person in the leg or buttocks [because] the idea of striking someone innocent, with inpunity, unprovoked, was the delicious thing—the compelling drug." He would be jailed, of course, and "there would follow, inevitably, shame and horror" (312). Although Dan is fifty-two years old, his daydreams are those of a boy with an air rifle; he admits that "most of all he adored himself as a boy" (313).

The subtheme of war enters the story as Dan drives his Riviera to visit Newt and Ivy, deciding to "give people a chance" because, as he remembers, he himself was once "a G-22, Intelligence, with the marines in the worst war ever, by *choice,* dim bulb in forehead. Whole squad smoked by mortars because of you," he tells himself. "Put them on the wrong beach. A gloomy competency would have been refreshing, ask their mothers" (322).

17. "Upstairs, Mona Bayed for Dong" originally appeared as "The Tyranny of the Visual" in *Southern Review* (University of Adelaide, Australia), (Autumn, 1992), 753–69; Bobbie Ann Mason, "Shiloh," in *"Shiloh" and Other Stories* (New York, 1982).

The comic irony of Dan's volunteering for "Intelligence," despite having a "dim bulb in [his] forehead," is undercut by the apparent serious consequences of his incompetence. Of course, Hannah protagonists never settle for a "gloomy competency" and look down upon those who do. Dan will soon realize his incompetence on a personal level.

Discovering that Ivy is a fine young woman and that his son Newt is "crazy, mean, unfinished," no longer writes poems, and finally disappears (324), Dan begins to look back at "whatever he'd left out, fathering the boy" (326). His depression over what he perceives as his failed parenting increases when old friends begin to die. Each death opens a painful memory: Dan and Chase had gone on a drunken binge after the G-22 misdirection of the Navy Seals; and just before Dan had left for Vietnam, he had last seen his high school classmate, Bridge, who was "in the National Guard . . . [and] had stolen from his unit a Browning .30-caliber machine gun and live ammo and enough gear to dress a store dummy" (328). The story, which alternates between Dan's memories and his present dilemma over his son, follows Newt as he becomes a convert to Mormonism and as he superintends a reform school where many of the boys are "large and dangerous" (340) and often attack him; yet Newt also writes new poems that are "extraordinary, going places glad and hellish he'd never approached before" (336). Every memory throws Dan back into his present battle for a coherent identity, particularly as a father. Because Newt identifies himself with such historically outcast groups as Mormons and Jews, and because he is eventually reconciled with his father, "Hey, Have You Got a Cig" might have been simply a contemporary prodigal son story. Closure comes, however, not with the reconciliation of father and son, in the mode of the epiphanic story, but with an additional scene in which after going fishing with Newt "in a pond so dark green and gorgeous you could forget the training school and human horror everywhere," Dan drives out of the complex and, with his Daisy, begins "popping the boys singly, aiming for the back of their necks and, if lucky, an ear . . . [so that they will] start asking some big questions" (341). Both the story's actual closure, which has Dan reverting to childish antics with his air rifle, and the penultimate idyllic father-son fishing scene ignore the fact that Newt, despite his alleged rehabilitation, continues his self-declared (self-inflicted?) martyrdom by remaining in a job in which he is repeatedly wounded by vicious, disturbed children. Thus, the cycle of adolescent violence is perpetuated in the lives of both father and son, precluding any epiphany or any real progress toward a stable identity for either.

In "That Was Close, Ma," Hannah writes another story set during the Desert Storm operation. This story is epistolary, a letter from a soldier to his mother; but the realism this form has historically been alleged to possess is made problematical by such comments as "You believe this?" (*BOH*, 356), and "The war has never concerned me, as war, so I should be the last trusted voice about whatever gallantry is ascribed to anybody" (357). Throughout the letter, which does indeed recount the teller's "gallantry," the self-reflexivity continues, with the soldier remarking, "It's pumping unusual things from me, this whole piece of writing," and "I am not going to write some long code to you about my feelings because I want it out in bright Mother Tongue on the page" (350). The two major themes are the act of writing and the self-initiation of the writer-narrator, who in racing unarmed behind enemy lines in full daylight enacts the equivalent of a Native American ritual known as "counting coup." The "coup" that is the aim of his derring-do is the taking of ceruba, a river root that can be found only in this dangerous fire zone but is required to make the favorite tea of Naomi Lee, an unlikely "prisoner of war from the other side . . . [who] has been turned around by our food and happiness" and has now been added to the American general's "harem" (345).

That the desert setting and the wild ride, albeit in an Army Rover, are meant to suggest the American West is upheld by the writer-protagonist's letter, which alludes not only to the Civil War but also to the violent American frontier, both the settings of daring raids on horseback. As if responding to incoming fire, he observes, conflating the twentieth-century war with the two nineteenth-century American experiences, "Very close and nasty, old friend. We had you in the scope very early. Oh Vicksburg, Vicksburg! I am, personally, the Fall of the West" (345). That Hannah sees the events of the story in the context of the American West is borne out by the title of the original story published in *Esquire:* "Rocket Launchers, Lust, Croquet, and the Fall of the West." Moreover, in his extensive revision of the story for inclusion in *Bats Out of Hell* as "That Was Close, Ma," Hannah included additional allusions to the Old West, such as the narrator's denigration of the Commander. On the second page of the later version of

the story, the clause "We imagine he could hit no better than the discred-
ited sheriffs of the Old West, and" prefaces the original sentence, which
read: "We imagine he required so many women because he never got it
right, he fouls it up time after time—the Uzi of sex" (346). The enlarged
sentence forms a separate emphatic paragraph, whereas the original sentence was the last in the previous paragraph, following the phrase "the fat
of the land." In the original story, the female prisoner of war was named
Newton Lee; the retitled version in *Bats Out of Hell* is much expanded and
heavily revised.[18]

One possible preclosure point in the story is the self-defining moment of
the hero, as he is cheered even by the enemy for his brave deed. The actual
closure, however, debunks any notion of a stable identity for this soldier, as
he relates his revenge upon the Commander, because "she was for *him*"
(355), a revenge accomplished when he changes the assault target imaging,
"doubl[ing] the image on the Commander's bunker . . . [so that] thirty
minutes later they hit him with at least three huge ones direct" (359). Finally, admitting that by this act he has sabotaged his own dream of heroism, he writes, "The things that create a traitor are really very simple, aren't
they, Ma?" (359). Naomi Lee, surviving the blast, smiles at him, "horror
still on her face," as if affirming his own self-assessment. His daring has
been insufficient to engender the heroic identity he longs for, and he remains a vindictive and "wretched . . . renegade" (360).

Debunking rhythms, as in "That Was Close, Ma," contribute to the
pervasive theme of initiation that accompanies the search for meaningful
male adulthood in all of Barry Hannah's stories. His unstable male protagonists are seeking some kind of reassurance in a world that has denied them
the comfort of a secure sense of self, often because they perceive threats to
or feel ambivalent about deeply desired human bonds. The initiation
theme is developed in a more general way in modern and contemporary
southern fiction in terms of a culturally enforced (learned and internalized)
idea of honor that is repeatedly shattered by the perverse human inability
to avoid shameful acts, as well as by a protagonist's ambivalence about the
culture's heroic myth and its demands. The psyche of a Hannah protago-

18. Barry Hannah, "Rocket Launchers, Lust, Croquet, and the Fall of the West," *Esquire*
(January, 1992), 82–84, 120–21.

nist, who is almost always male, is fragmented by a betrayal or by a breach that touches on his identity. Consequently, the narrative structures of the stories that reveal these psychic ruptures are repeatedly fragmented by the disjunctive thoughts of a narrator or the consciousness of a central character who must constantly admit that as he schemes and plots to gain fame in his search for honor, love, and/or power, his behavior is self-contradictory—infamous. These characters live by their imaginations, for their lives are fictions of their own creation and re-creation.

As "That Was Close, Ma" shows, Hannah's fiction continually debunks not only fraudulent individual pretensions but also fraudulent cultural demands that contribute to the angst that contemporary men and women often lie to conceal and also try to subvert or manipulate in some way, just to survive. One of the most insidious cultural imperatives is the American cult of youth, which can cause an identity crisis in the middle-aged, as it does for Vaughtie and Nick in "Upstairs, Mona Bayed for Dong." Vaughtie, in fact, carries a card in her purse on which she has written a quotation from J. M. Barrie, the author of *Peter Pan:* "Nothing that happens after we are twelve matters very much"; and Nick asks himself, "Are we all alas just obsolete children?" (*BOH,* 269).

In "Get Some Young," the lead story of his latest collection, *High Lonesome,* Hannah depicts the modern psyche that succumbs to the contemporary cult of youth, in a postmodern parable of the so-called dysfunctional family whose obsessions drive them into more and more aberrant behavior.[19] Integral to the story is a self-questioning narrative that distinguishes it from modernist mimesis. Tuck, the narrator of the opening paragraphs of the story, is having a midlife crisis. We are told that he "loved his wife, but no he didn't" (29). A forty-one-year-old veteran, Tuck has, since Korea, lived with Bernadette "in mutual disregard, which turned three times a month into animal passion then diminished on the sharp incline to hatred, at last collecting in time into silent equal fatigue" (3). Tuck wears a beard, behind which he "believed that his true expressions were hidden" (3). He is taunted by the young boys and girls who come into his store and, jealous of their youth, wonders if he "wishe[s] to wear their bodies as a younger self"

19. Barry Hannah's "Get Some Young" was first published in *Reckon: The Magazine of Southern Culture,* I (1995), 128–39.

(4). The story, then, presents itself as a quest for eternal youth and lost innocence, in which the protagonist tries to create an innocent self; it is the
fiction of a fiction. Moreover, the characters are voyeurs who cannot escape
one another's gaze but who also try to disguise themselves, so that the narrative is a collage of scenes, each seemingly intended to upstage the other,
and of actors "acting like grown-ups" or "hungry for an act" (10). When
the boys are drunk on peach wine they think about "serious acts never
acted, women never had" (23). Throughout the story, Hannah puns on the
concept of "the act," which ultimately refers to the act of sex, and which
Tuck associates with youth and sees personified in Swanly, as "this happy
thing all might have come to." The narrator declares, "It ain't pondering or
chatting or wishing it's only the act, from dog to man to star all nature
either exploding or getting ready to" (15). Thus, the story's title becomes
an ironic double inversion of the modern adolescent's desire to "get some
[sex while] young," by implying also the aging couple's wish to "get
some [sex from the] young," by which process they mean to "get [regain]
some [youth]."

The third-person narrative of "Get Some Young" alternates between the
central consciousness of Tuck and that of Swanly, one of five boys who
camp out near his country store and through whom Tuck lives vicariously.
Each time Tuck submerges himself in his young alter ego, form becomes
substance as the narrative shifts and the incongruous juxtapositions rein-
force the depiction of his unstable personality. Swanly's sense of self is also
elusive and perhaps illusory. Because he is as "graceful as a tennis player"
(5), Swanly is seen by Tuck as a beautiful, heroic figure; yet the boy himself
alternates between feeling that he is "bred out of a golden mare with a saber
in his hand" and that he is "ugly, out of an ass" (8). The language used to
express his feelings points to the story's intertextuality and its generic mixture, both of which undermine its mimetic coherence. The centaurlike
"mare with a saber in his hand" is itself a grotesque mixed breed, which
combines here with a fairytale alter ego, an "ugly . . . ass." The mare image
has meaning on several intertextual levels, since the saber, a symbol that for
Hannah usually represents the weapon of a Confederate officer and thus
implies nineteenth-century historic (real) time, is conflated with fabulous
monsters from the mythic (timeless) realm. Hannah's intertextuality is so
pervasive that even seemingly throwaway lines, such as "thief of time" (14),

which Tuck calls the hermit-voyeur, Sunballs, who spies on everyone from a bluff overlooking the river, link this story with Nabokov's *Pale Fire* and, beyond that, to Shakespeare's *Timon of Athens,* as well as to the theme of time. Moreover, the boy's simultaneous self-images of "ass" and "mare" involve gender confusion, while the narrative confirms that in his sexual immaturity Swanly is "all boy but between genders" (29). Since he is "a prescient boy" (5), Swanly's consciousness is a confused mixture: he is at the same time "blithe in his boy ways" and fearful of "the foul gloom of job and woman ahead" (7). He foresees his own impending lost youth; indeed, evidence of his fate is all around him in the story's ironic contrasts. It is especially evident in the extended river scene in which the nude Swanly, "like a piece of languid Attic statuary" (24), is contrasted with the hermit, who is "the color of organic decay" (25). That Sunballs is eventually blinded for his voyeurism foregrounds the Oedipal subtext of the story.

Another of the story's subtexts is its emotional basis in the fiction of Hemingway, not only in the similar themes of time and lost innocence but also in major symbols like the wounded male and the corrupting female and in allusions to specific Hemingway stories. For example, Tuck is depressed by the aging of his sons as he "watch[es] visible time on them, the horrible millions of minutes collected and evident, the murdered idle thousands of hours" (28); he wants to "live backwards in time" until he looks like Swanly (29). Like many a Hemingway hero, Tuck is literally wounded when, in a fit of pique, he runs out of the house at night and "neck[s] himself" on a clothesline wire in the back yard (10). The contaminating influence of woman is apparent when Bernadette visits the "motherless pirates" with a picnic lunch, much as Wendy came to Peter Pan's lost boys (24); they feel that "their sanctuary [has been] ruined . . . [by] Big Mama Busybod . . . Courtesy of the Southern regions . . . [and that] there will always be a woman around to wreck things" (26). The obvious source of the language that describes them as boys with "big hearts" (4) who fish, drink, and play with guns in the Strong River is Hemingway's "Big Two-Hearted River," a story also known for its antithetical rhythms and recalcitrant narrative, as Leitch points out. When the five become eloquent on peach wine, Walthall, the poet of the group, who plays "inept but solemn chamber music" on viola "with his root floating in the rills" (24–25) and who wears "a necklace of twine and long mail-order Mauser shells" (23), declaims a collage of allusions, including "Send not to ask for when the bell tolls" (23). Indeed, in this story, it tolls continuously, and for all.[20]

Tuck is tormented by a love for Swanly that is partly paternal, as he compares him with his own sons, and partly self-love, for he sees in the boy his own lost youth. When Swanly and Tuck's wife fall in love right before his eyes, Tuck merges his vision in Swanly's, so that he sees Bernadette anew, as "a right holy wonder" (21). Bernadette, the fallen madonna with the name of a saint, also re-creates her life through an imaginative merging with Swanly, in a mental fiction of immaculate conception. As she ponders her sons, who "were hammy and homely . . . she wander[s] in a moment of conception, giving birth to Swanly all over again as he stood there, a pained ecstasy in the walls of her womb. He was what she had intended by everything female about her" (21). Man and wife achieve a new union in this "boy savior" (33). When the ménage à trois retires for the night, they are described as an American parody of the Holy Family: "In this trinity already a pact was sealed and they could no more be like others. There was a tingling and a higher light around them. A flood of goodwill took her as if they had been hurled upon a foreign shore, all fresh. The boy savior, child, and paramour at once" (33).

Sentimental nostalgia for boyhood is mixed with a bizarre literary naturalism in "Get Some Young," a story that begins as a fantasy in which the innocence of youth is called upon to renew the jaded love of Tuck and Bernadette. Tuck laments his loss of any proper sense of self, which he identifies with his lost youth, complaining that during the Korean War his "own boyself was eat up by the gooks and then this strolling wench, my boyself was hostaged by her" (29). But in his love for Swanly he feels renewed; he "feel[s] love for [his wife] all over again" (30), and their night begins with idyllic images of a recaptured Eden. When she looks at Tuck, Bernadette now sees "another man, fluent, [who] had risen in his place"; she declares it "a true morning out of all the rest of the mornings" (35). During this process, Tuck and Bernadette are the principal actors, whereas Swanly is a passive initiate into the mysteries of adult sex, an adolescent fantasy shared by

20. Leitch, "The Debunking Rhythm," in *Short Story Theory at a Crossroads,* ed. Lohafer and Clarey, 132.

all the boys and voiced by Walthall: "Lord my right one for mature love like that" (31).

Had the story ended at this point, the genre would indeed be that of fantasy. But what has begun as a dream of love turns into nightmare for all, including Swanly's young friends, who witness the violent end to the grotesque charade and see in it their own fate: "[Swanly's] beauty had been a strange thing. It had always brought on some distress and then infinite kindness in others and then sadness too. But none of them were cherubs any longer and they knew all this and hated it, seeing him now across the woman's lap, her breasts over his twisted face. Eden in the bed of Eros, all Edenwide all lost" (39). Hannah is playing on major archetypal images from several traditions and turning them all inside out, including those from Greek mythology and Judeo-Christian typology, the latter particularly as expressed in the literature of the American dream. Here is the innocent American Adam initiated anew into the Fall by an already fallen twentieth-century Adam and Eve, in a "wilderness" adulterated by a convenience store typical of New South "progress." The grotesque three-way relationship has been foreshadowed by Walthall's description of them as "a six-legged crippled thing" (34), and the Oedipal moral judgment for their effective incest is apparent in the description of a sickly Swanly in its aftermath as "blind" (40) and in "exile" (41).

"Get Some Young," in which innocent campers are violated by lascivious adults, is as symbolic of the American dream turned nightmare as is Hawthorne's "My Kinsman, Major Molineux," a nineteenth-century depiction of the innocent adolescent's initiation into the experience of human sin and also, as in Hannah's story, of "all [American] Edenwide all lost." It is thus a retelling, in human terms, of repeated violations of the pristine American wilderness. Moreover, in "Get Some Young," the juxtaposition of so many incongruous elements combines with the continuous punning and inverted, debunking closure to create a parody of the initiation plot. Bernadette suckles the boy "in a condition of the Pietà" (38), his face "twisted" (39), his very youth drained from him by her and Tuck's vampirelike desires, in a scene that parodies not only that of the young mother who gives her saving breast milk to an old man at the conclusion of John Steinbeck's *Grapes of Wrath* but also many artistic depictions of the pietà of

Mary and Jesus. In Hannah's grotesque pietà, the image of Swanly's limp body draped across Bernadette's lap is as distorted as are the anatomies of figures in many of the classic paintings of Christ's deposition from the cross. When his friends come to take Swanly away, in a bizarre literary parody of the deposition, Bernadette makes a pseudo-prelapsarian protest: "We were good people," which Tuck amends with a postlapsarian self-judgment: "We are bad. . . . Damn us, damn it all" (40). The brief but audacious scene, which also conjures images of the eternally aging Tiresias and of Oscar Wilde's *Picture of Dorian Gray,* seems to break up into so many mythic and other allusive directions that it is the very antithesis of coherent modernist myth structure. Indeed, a Hannah story constitutes the kind of text that Roland Barthes called a "multidimensional space in which a variety of writings, none of them original, blend and clash." Such polyvocality, which underlies antithesis in Hannah's fiction, is but one of the attributes that mark it as postmodernist. Lance Olsen notes the dual significance to postmodernism of June 22, 1986, the date when "the *New York Times Book Review* ran a front-page essay by Denis Donoghue called 'The Promiscuous Cool of Postmodernism'": (1) that "one of the most popular newspapers of the literary establishment decided to say it too had seen the unicorn and had decided to pass on the Word to its general readership"; and (2) that "with the appearance of his essay the culture at large suddenly acknowledged, if not wholly endorsed, the concept of the postmodern." During the height of the postmodernist period, in the 1970s, Hannah began to publish stories characterized by "the promiscuous cool of postmodernism."[21]

Antithetical technique prevails in "Get Some Young" at the level of language also. For example, Hannah not only combines elevated and vulgar diction but also conflates passages from several Dylan Thomas poems, including two in a single sentence, to produce Walthall's sardonic toast, "Do not go gently in my sullen craft, up yours" (23). In the bargain, Hannah manages to pun on "craft," which here suggests a boat but which in Thomas' poem "In My Craft or Sullen Art" alludes as well to the craft of poetry. There are also incongruous juxtapositions, such as a drunken boy's

21. Roland Barthes, *Image, Music, Text,* trans. Stephen Heath (New York, 1977), 146; Lance Olsen, *Circus of the Mind in Motion: Postmodernism and the Comic Vision* (Detroit, 1990), 25.

vomiting described as if it were the miracle of the rainbow occurring in the midst of *Moby-Dick:* "Pal could swallow no more and heaved out an arc of puke luminous over the fire, crying, Thar she blows, my dear youth. This act was witnessed like a miracle by the others" (33).

In a deferred and anticlimactic closure that tells what has happened to the main characters "some 14 years later" (41), the style is that of romance, a mode in which poetic justice usually prevails. One thinks of the conclusion of Charlotte Brontë's *Jane Eyre,* not only because of the downfall of Hannah's "villains" but also because the contrast with the preceding passage's narrative style is almost as great as if Hannah had written "Dear Reader." The content, however, is neither romantic nor epiphanic at the end of this tale of suburban death and madness, because the conclusion counters reader expectations established by the early images of Eden and adolescent initiation. The final note is sounded when Walthall, one of the five friends, has returned to ask "the whereabouts of Swanly" and is answered only by the screams of the "clearly mad old woman . . . behind the cash register . . . wearing Swanly's old jersey, what was left of it" (41). After the debacle, Walthall, the artist character in the story who is now "rich but sad . . . [and] struck by a nostalgia that he could not account for" (41), has, like the Ancient Mariner, escaped into the world to tell the story. The ordering of the story is based on a process that consists not in the mimesis of but in the "unmaking" of a coherent identity, as its darkly ambiguous ending scream withholds a final revelation.

Hannah employs similar structures in most of his short stories and also in his novellas, the condensed and recalcitrant nature of which make them much closer to poetry than to the novel. His narratives perform what Mikhail M. Bakhtin calls a verbal and semantic "decenter[ing] of the ideological world, a certain linguistic homelessness of literary consciousness, which no longer possesses a sacrosanct and unitary linguistic medium for containing ideological thought." In other words, a Hannah narrative is not customarily built around one coherent center, one controlling image or theme, such as initiation into adulthood; rather, his narratives present a collage of several possible thematic and structural centers, each of which overlaps the other at odd angles in Hannah's "unstable area of textual play," to repeat Ian Reid's phrase. In "Get Some Young," the wilderness setting is a stage but not a cover for a strange mixture of evil and innocence, hope and fear; an inverted initiation of adults into youth results in the premature aging of the youth; a Christ/Adonis figure is seduced by an Eve/Madonna who wishes to give herself a new birth through him; and an Oedipal nightmare of alienation fades into a dream of innocence but rematerializes more desolate than ever. These elements converge with images of acts and acting, visions and voyeurs, stories and tellers, imaginations gone wild beyond rational explanation in characters who are—or become—interesting monsters. Perhaps the greatest disjunction of all is the ironic humor that derives from the juxtaposition of tragic events presented with such exuberant linguistic play.[22]

The disjunctions in contemporary society are often the subject of metafiction, specifically what Raymond Federman in 1975 called "surfiction," to denote a verbal surrealism; it is within this mode that Mark Charney places the stories of Hannah's *Captain Maximus*. Federman defines surfiction in terms of its eccentric visual presentation; its digressive, self-questioning, nonlinear, even chaotic narrative; and its characters without fixed or stable identities, who may even be illusory, and all of whom may converge in a split protagonist, often an author-participant. Surfictional texts are not intended to carry an absolute meaning, Federman says, but they may have a meaning "extracted" by readers who are able to join their imaginations with the writer's. Indeed, since many of these characteristics are but extensions of modernist experimentations, they are evident in much contemporary fiction, although usually in ways less radical than their manifestations in the work of surfictionists like Vladimir Nabokov, John Barth, Raymond Federman, and Ronald Sukenick. Like surfiction, Hannah's fiction "tries to explore the possibilities of fiction . . . [by] challeng[ing] the tradition that governs it . . . constantly renews our faith in man's imagination and not in man's distorted vision of reality . . . reveals man's irrationality rather than man's rationality . . . [and] exposes the fictionality of reality." That Hannah's fiction is in some sense autobiographical only adds to its surfictional character, since it illustrates Federman's premise that "the experience of life gains meaning only in its recounted form."[23]

22. Mikhail M. Bakhtin, *The Dialogic Imagination,* trans. Caryl Emerson and Michael Holquist (Austin, 1981), 367.

23. Charney, *Barry Hannah,* 70–71; Raymond Federman, "Surfiction—Four Propositions in the Form of an Introduction," in *Surfiction: Fiction Now . . . and Tomorrow,* ed. Federman (Chicago, 1975), 7–14.

Hannah's short stories, as well as his novels, employ several varieties of recalcitrance, levels of obscurity that often characterize but are not limited to metafiction. Hannah's admittedly complex narratives are more accessible than most metafiction, for even those narratives most obviously in the border zone between fact and fiction are recognized as belonging to the category of "story," as opposed to more ambiguous postcontemporary designations such as "text" or "work." Barry Hannah is first of all a storyteller, whose stories' obscure, nonlinear, and unresolved structures, as well as their orality and general intertextuality, mark them as part of the antithetical lyric tradition that continues to modify American modernism. Although genre theorists Douglas Hesse and Austin M. Wright have observed that American short fiction is no longer developing in the direction of radical metafiction, Hannah is one of the most important contemporary writers who continue to revitalize recognized narrative traditions, giving us new ways to see human truth by appropriating some of metafiction's antimimetic strategies.[24]

The debunking rhythm of Barry Hannah's fiction, then, is one narrative technique that identifies him with the larger movement of postmodernism. An important part not only of the American but also of the international postmodern "enterprise" has been, since the 1960s, the task of "bridging the 'real' and the 'fictive,' or the familiar and the unfamiliar," according to Malcolm Bradbury. Responding to Tom Wolfe's claim that *Bonfire of the Vanities* is an attempt to counter postmodern "self-regarding experiments . . . [such as] absurdist novels, magic realist novels . . . [and] minimalist novels," Bradbury, in a 1992 *Times Literary Supplement* article, shows their similar sociological bent in his survey of literary trends since the "parodic funhouse" era of American fiction in the 1960s and 1970s, when "the *scriptible* prevailed." Bradbury sees the Latin American and Eastern European literary experiments, with their "widening fund of narrative resources and aesthetic mixtures, and [their] growing sense of the fantastic or hyperreal as themselves powers within history, aspects of reality." In this essay, entitled "Closer to Chaos: American Fiction in the 1980s," which describes a time when "postmodern fiction seem[s] to move ever closer towards the absurd reality," Bradbury traces the movement from "pre-postmoderns"

---

24. Douglas Hesse, "A Boundary Zone: First-Person Short Stories and Narrative Essays," in *Short Story Theory at a Crossroads,* ed. Lohafer and Clarey, 105; Wright, "Recalcitrance in the Short Story," *ibid.,* 129.

like Bellow, Philip Roth, Mailer, and Updike to the literature depicting the "fast-food counter, the shopping mall, the trailer park . . . [and other] alienations of a media-dominated and commodified age" in Raymond Carver, Richard Ford, and Tobias Wolff; to the "surreal banality" of Don DeLillo; and, although postmodernism had at first seemed "a male affair," to the Vietnam nightmares in Bobbie Ann Mason's *In Country* and Jayne Anne Phillips' *Machine Dreams.* These contemporary and postcontemporary American writers are creating a new kind of social realism, Bradbury says, whose narrative surfaces tend to conceal a basis in the urban novels of Theodore Dreiser, John Dos Passos, and James Farrell, and, ultimately, in Thomas Wolfe's *You Can't Go Home Again,* all fictions whose roots are in the nineteenth-century social novel. Bradbury is repudiating the latter-day Tom Wolfe's claim that his journalistic *Bonfire of the Vanities* should be the model for American fiction rather than the novels of the 1980s, which Wolfe sees as escapes from reality. In arguing that today's fiction does not "let contemporary social reality slip away out of sight," Bradbury does not name Barry Hannah. Hannah, however, is at home in the company Bradbury cites, and he shares the general postmodernist concern with the representation of a social reality that presents itself as absurd and chaotic.[25]

Amid the chaos of Hannah's fictional representations, there are important points of coherence. Michael Spikes, while acknowledging that both the narrative and the narrator of *Ray* are "on one level, shot through with discontinuities," nevertheless sees Ray as an artist figure who "formulates, from his dealings with various representational forms, a principle of aesthetic unity and meaning which he enacts in his own art in order to anchor and consolidate his inconsistent thoughts and behavior." Another point of coherence is found in the dialogue of a Hannah story, even in the disagreements within the story and between the story and its background of cultural myths, often including the emerging mythology of Vietnam. This coherence is based on the play of mind and memory instead of on the development of plot and character. Much of Hannah's fiction is of a piece with other Vietnam literature that, in Beidler's words, is set in "a place with no real points of reference, then *or* now. As once in experiential fact, so now

---

25. Malcolm Bradbury, "Closer to Chaos: American Fiction in the 1980s," *Times Literary Supplement,* May 22, 1991, pp. 17–18.

in memory as well." Like the writers Beidler describes, Hannah creates a landscape "that never was, . . . a landscape of consciousness where it might be possible to accommodate experience remembered within a new kind of imaginative cartography endowing it with large configurings of value and signification." Such a landscape of consciousness lends itself to the growing tendency to see the South as more like the rest of the country, as Robert Brinkmeyer, Jr., notes in his analysis of Mason's *In Country,* a book that "prob[ed] the darker sides of our national experience," in which "her focus is less on the Southern experience than on the American, and so for her a Southerner's quest for self-definition means coming to terms with America and not the South . . . [a] focus that leads her back to the era of the Vietnam War, a period that tested the American way of life from within and without." Although their plot curves and settings are, without question, obscure because of poetic compression and stylization, Hannah's stories partake of American literary traditions, in both content and structure. He writes, as do most southern writers, a literature of place; but unlike most southern literature, the "place" is not always a tangible locale. "Get Some Young," for example, has a general southern ambiance, but its power in no way depends on regional effect; it could be set anywhere. Especially in the war stories, a primary component of Hannah's fiction is an intellectualized landscape similar to that which Beidler recalls in the journals of early American colonists, such as Cotton Mather, and in the fiction of Charles Brockden Brown, J. Fenimore Cooper, and Nathaniel Hawthorne. These authors found, in the New World, "a dim, beckoning path of discovery and sacrifice and bloodshed and terror . . . [in the] dark woods, the swamps, the mountains, the rivers, the 'howling wilderness.' "[26]

Hannah, like others who write war into literature, finds just such a "beckoning path" in the emotional and intellectual consequences of both the American Civil War and the Vietnam conflict, and his stories explore possible meanings along this path. In form, they exhibit neither the unity afforded by a climactic plot structure nor a clear epiphany, yet the content

26. Michael P. Spikes, "What's in a Name? A Reading of Barry Hannah's *Ray,*" *Mississippi Quarterly,* XLII (1988–89), 71, 73; Beidler, *American Literature and the Experience of Vietnam,* 16, 22, Beidler's emphasis; Robert H. Brinkmeyer, Jr., "Finding One's History: Bobbie Ann Mason and Contemporary Southern Literature," *Southern Literary Journal,* XIX (1987), 32.

of each war story challenges thoughtful readers in several ways. As Kenneth Seib argues about the J. E. B. Stuart stories, Hannah's narrators search for meaning in ways that not only demythicize the legendary Confederate hero but also reject the macho warrior image with which southern men have historically identified. Thus Hannah deglamorizes the mythology of war and the myth of the warrior, even while exhibiting Americans' fascination with both, and while dispelling the illusion that even the most devoutly held, most pervasive and seductive, cultural ideals and models can engender in any individual aspirant a truly unified self based on them. Perhaps the reader's greatest challenge is to understand that many of Hannah's stories cohere around the antiphonal, often cacophonic, debunking rhythms that contribute to the debunking of the unitary self and story.[27]

27. Seib, " 'Sabers, Gentlemen, Sabers,' " 41–52.

THREE

Storytellers and Other Interesting Monsters: From Oral History to Postmodern Narrative

All people who achieve things are sort of monsters. . . . I write about interesting monsters.
—Barry Hannah, interviewed by Tom Vitale

The popular-festive system of images . . . is most clearly expressed in carnival. . . . In such a system the king is the clown . . . [to be] abused and beaten when the time of his reign is over, just as the carnival dummy of winter or of the dying year is mocked, beaten, torn to pieces, burned, or drowned. . . . They are "gay monsters."
—M. M. Bakhtin, *Rabelais and His World*

THE "INTERESTING MONSTERS" Hannah says he writes about are sometimes obvious descendants of Sherwood Anderson's "grotesques," which Anderson defined in "The Book of the Grotesque," the preface to *Winesburg, Ohio;* thus they are typical of the literature of psychological realism. "Hundreds and hundreds were the truths and they were all beautiful," says the narrator of "The Book of the Grotesque," describing the theory of his writer-protagonist, and "the moment one of the people took one of the truths to himself, called it his truth, and tried to live by it, he became a grotesque and the truth he embraced became a falsehood." In this vein, Hannah's grotesques are characters with distorted visions, often obsessed with one idea. An unmistakable tribute to Anderson is the explicit allusion to "Death in the Woods" in Hannah's "Two Gone Over," in which the narrator describes a woman as being "like something from the heart of winter in a foreign land. Same old story full of wolves where you'd stumble into a woman lying in the woods. I'm going to use a word. *Alabaster*" (*HL,* 184). And like such Anderson stories as "Death in the Woods," Hannah's fiction calls attention to itself as artifact. However, unlike the characters of Anderson or those of writers he influenced, such as Hemingway, Hannah's behave in ways that oppose their stated "truths." If obsessed with spousal fidelity, they are unfaithful; if convinced of the superiority of women, they degrade women; if obsessed with truth itself, they are liars; with honor, they act dishonorably. Many despise their own ordinariness even as they yearn for some "maximum" experience that might lift them out of it.[1]

At the opposite extreme in Hannah's cast of characters are true monsters: legendary or supernatural creatures whose visitations reveal their uncanny relation to the human monsters who also inhabit his stories. Somewhere in between are those who commit monstrous, bizarre acts, from the murderer in *Nightwatchmen* to the "lout named Reggy John," who has tied "his supposed sweetheart . . . underneath a bull with rope, all naked" in "Quo Vadis, Smut?" (*A,* 67). All are apparently responding in outrage to an absurd world; and even these, as they flail about in search of a stable self-image, however out of control, however despicable, represent an aspect of the "wildness"—Hannah's term for creative originality—that he champions. In a 1993 radio interview with Tom Vitale, Hannah said he believes that there is "too much uniformity [and] not enough wildness in men and women." Fred Hobson's comments in *The Southern Writer in the Postmodern World* are helpful in understanding Hannah's aversion to such uniformity in the Sunbelt South, which, with its ubiquitous shopping malls, is now so much like the rest of the country. Hobson describes writers' various adaptations, in the 1970s and 1980s, to a South much the opposite of the "defeated, failed, poor, guilt-ridden, tragic" South of Faulkner. He argues that "a suddenly Superior South, optimistic, forward-looking, more virtuous and now threatening to become more prosperous than the rest of the

1. Sherwood Anderson, *Winesburg, Ohio* (1919; rpr. New York, 1960), 23–24.

country" is a reality accepted by most contemporary southern writers—but not by Hannah. To Hannah, Hobson says, this homogeneous suburban world is "bizarre for all its trappings of civilization." Against this world of unthinking sameness and calcified stereotypes Hannah's wild and unruly characters rage, appearing as monsters in comparison with the maddening "herd," to use a word Hannah likes.[2]

These contemporary rebel "screamers" are integral to the philosophic content of Hannah's fiction, for not only is it marked by many of the features often listed as characteristic of a postmodern poetics, which David Lodge describes in terms of "contradiction, discontinuity, randomness, excess, short circuit"; it also reflects the shift from the dominant epistemological concern of modernism to the dominant ontological concern of postmodernism. To use Dick Higgins' comparison, where the modernist may ask, "How can I interpret this world of which I am a part? And what am I in it?" the postmodernist asks instead not about knowing but about being in the world. The postmodernist's questions, which Higgins calls "post-cognitive," are most often "Which world is this? What is to be done in it? Which of my selves is to do it?" Brian McHale, in his survey of postmodernist poetics, is quick to add that epistemological and ontological questions are closely related, one implying the other, and that "the function of the dominant . . . [concern is that] it specifies the *order* in which different aspects are to be attended to. . . . In postmodernist texts, in other words, epistemology is *backgrounded,* as the price for foregrounding ontology." Hannah's emphasis on modes of being constitutes an oblique but unmistakable criticism of a society that discourages original modes and thus original beings, who are stigmatized as the very monsters that Hannah admires, who ask wrong (outrageous) questions, to which they find no socially acceptable answers.[3]

Hannah's characters are nothing if not original beings, and their lionization of the heroes they consider even more original is an integral part of

2. Tom Vitale, Interview with Barry Hannah, *A Moveable Feast,* Radio Series Broadcast #9403 (1993), rpr. on audiotape as *Barry Hannah Reads Stories from His Collection "Bats Out of Hell"* (Columbia, Mo., 1993); Fred Hobson, *The Southern Writer in the Postmodern World* (Athens, Ga., 1991), 8–9.

3. David Lodge and Dick Higgins, quoted in Brian McHale, *Postmodernist Fiction* (London, 1987), 7, 10; McHale, *ibid.,* 11, emphasis McHale's.

their personalities. In "Return to Return," a story published in *Esquire* in 1975, he creates two characters that illustrate the pattern and that will continue to engage his imagination through the story's revision for *Airships* (1978) to its final form as the opening chapter in his novella *The Tennis Handsome* (1983). The subtitle of the original story, "Base Line to Net and the Dead Run Back," identifies its setting in the world of tennis and continues the title's pun on the tennis handsome's "supernatural" tendency to return from the dead.[4]

In the story's first two appearances, its opening paragraph describes French Edward, the tennis star who is the object of hero worship and exploitation by Dr. "Baby" Levaster, former high school tennis star, sometime physician, and now manager of French Edward. Both early versions begin: "They used to call French Edward the happiest man on the court, and the prettiest. The crowds hated to see him beaten. Women anguished to conceive of his departure from a tournament. Once, when Edward lost a dreadfully long match at Forest Hills, an old man in the audience roared with sobs, then female voices joined his. It was like seeing the death of Mercutio or Hamlet, going down with a resigned smile" (*A,* 67). In *The Tennis Handsome,* although the book title refers to French Edward, what had occupied the second paragraph in the earlier versions now opens the book, introducing not the hero but the middle-aged hero worshiper: "Dr. Levaster drove the Lincoln. It was rusty and the valves stuck. On the rear floorboard two rainpools sloshed, disturbing the mosquitoes that rode the beer cans. The other day he became forty. His hair was thin, his eyes swollen beneath sunglasses, his ears small and red. Yet he was not monstrous, or very ugly. He seemed, actually, to have just retreated from some untowardness" (*TH,* 3).

After reframing the comic pair in terms of Hannah's revised dual focus on French Edward, the athlete as "interesting monster," and his primary fan, who "was not monstrous," the opening chapter of *The Tennis Handsome* segues to the description of the hero, with an addition that emphasizes French Edward's style over substance and thus his actual mock-heroic status: "The man with him was a few years younger, built well, curly passionate hair, face dashed with sun. His name was French Edward, the tennis

4. Barry Hannah, "Return to Return: Base Line to Net and the Dead Run Back," *Esquire* (October, 1975), 160–65.

pro. They used to call him the happiest man on the court, and the prettiest. *He had more style losing than L. or N. or S. did winning.* The crowds hated to see French Edward beaten" (*TH,* 3; emphasis added). From that early story, *The Tennis Handsome* is a spinoff that follows the lives of four natives of Vicksburg, Mississippi: French Edward; Baby Levaster; Dr. James Word, professor of botany and college tennis coach; and Bobby Smith, who had appeared as the protagonist in the *Esquire* and *Airships* versions of "Midnight and I'm Not Famous Yet," and whose story of unheroic action in Vietnam and its aftermath reappears in Chapter 2 of *The Tennis Handsome* and continues to weave in and out of the novel. Smith's story intersects that of the tennis crowd when he appears as a fan and eventual hanger-on of the tennis star, whose name had been John Whitelaw in the earlier versions of "Midnight."[5]

French Edward's larger-than-life status derives not only from his prowess on the court but also from his apparent ability to defeat death in several consecutive revivifications: after he apparently drowns when he goes "off the midpoint of the Mississippi Bridge at Vicksburg . . . either trying to save or trying to drown his old tennis coach, Doctor Word" (*TH,* 5); after "lightning strike[s his] racquet, blow[ing] it out of his hands" during a match (75); and after he attempts to "recharge . . . himself off a bus battery" (128). Such adventures convince French Edward that he can "walk on water" (4), but what seems to reinvigorate him physically also enervates his already weak intellect. Thus, Hannah presents the tournament-hopping tennis hero as a supernaturally victorious questing knight and Levaster, his feckless manager, as the "wisdom" figure who does his thinking for him. Both are parodies of figures from heroic fantasy. Tzvetan Todorov explains the significance of such figures in medieval texts, such as *The Quest of the Holy Grail:* "The possessors of meaning form a special category among the characters: they are 'sages,' hermits, abbots, and recluses. Just as the knights could not *know,* these . . . [sages] cannot *act.*"[6]

Hannah foreshadows his use of the archetypal pair by presenting French Edward as one who cannot *know.* Early in *The Tennis Handsome,* for example, Levaster declares that his protégé "has no mind outside of me" (8);

5. Barry Hannah, "Midnight and I'm Not Famous Yet," *Esquire* (July, 1975), 58–60+.

6. Tzvetan Todorov, *The Poetics of Prose,* trans. Richard Howard (Ithaca, N.Y., 1977), 122–23.

later, when French asks, "You mean I can't have a thought?" Baby answers, "You could have one, but it wouldn't last for very long" (29). After French attempts the rescue of the suicidal James Word, we are told that he "had drowned and had broken one leg, but had crawled out of the water anyhow. But his brain was damaged" (36). During a match at the Longwood Cricket Club in Boston, Levaster muses upon previous "kind . . . mentions" of the tennis star by sportscaster Bud Collins, wondering if there might still be "a place in his heart and ear for an aging, handsome *moron* of the tennis world" (*TH,* 75; emphasis added). It is impossible to say whether Hannah had the knight and sage characters in mind during the writing. However, he heavily edited the earlier *Airships* story for inclusion in *The Tennis Handsome,* tightening the narrative, paring away redundancies, and honing the language for greater precision. One significant change removed a description of French Edward that would have undermined the archetype. In the *Airships* version, the tennis handsome "had become a spoiler against high seeds in early rounds, though never a winner. His style was greatly admired. . . . Madrid [newspapers] said, 'He fights windmills, but, viewing his style, we are convinced his contests matter.' . . . Then it occurred to Levaster. French had never been humiliated in a match. . . . The handsome head had never bowed, the rusting gold of French Edward's curls stayed high in the sun. He remained the *sage* and brute that he was when he was nineteen" (*A,* 90–91; emphasis added). In *The Tennis Handsome* version of this passage, everything after "his contests matter" is replaced by the sentence "*Certainement,* thought Levaster" (31), with the epithet "sage" no longer used to describe French Edward, whose task is "fight[ing] windmills" on the tennis circuit. Thus, he parodies Don Quixote, a knight character; it is for him to *act,* not to *know.* Furthermore, he is an "interesting monster" not only because he repeatedly defies death but also because, as only one half of a narrative device, he is incomplete: he is the physical (acting) half, along with his (thinking) alter ego, Baby Levaster, of a split character. He is both more and less than fully human.

Ned Maximus, the protagonist of "Ride, Fly, Penetrate, Loiter," who is called "Maximum Ned," is an important early prototype of Hannah's characters with a fixation on greatness; many of the stories in *Captain Maximus,* in which Ned's story is central, depict the mock-hero who wishes he were a real hero. Ned is the quintessential Hannah character: a middle-aged Mis-

sissippi male, "a drunk who is raving with bad attitudes" (*CM,* 36), a liar
who hates fakes and frauds, who is alienated from his wife, who identifies
with weapons, who is his own worst enemy, and who is a writer. Ned is always "wanting some hero for a buddy: somebody who would attack the
heart of the night with me" (36). "Ride, Fly, Penetrate, Loiter" begins
when "a fake Indian named Billy Seven Fingers . . . [who] might be goug-
ing the Feds with thirty-second-part maximum Indian blood" stabs a
drunken Ned in the eye with Ned's own fish knife. However, countering
the negative aspects of Ned's personality is his wildness, which is presented
as positive; leaving Tuscaloosa on his Triumph motorcycle, without a gun,
he is high not only on the painkillers he has taken for his wound but also, as
he says, on "my own personal natural dope running in me" (37). This story,
which includes much in its spirit that is autobiographical and some details
that are oblique autobiographical referents, includes a ride across the southwestern desert that alludes both to Eliot's *The Waste Land* and to a low
(dry) period in Hannah's life. Like Hannah himself, Ned is first of all a
writer. He sees out of his remaining eye with "penetrating clarity" (37); and
"under the patch," he claims, his eye "burns deep for language. I will write
sometimes and my bones hurt" (38). Twice we hear disclaimers about the
truth of stories; yet, these disclaimers are contained in a story within the
frame story, and are introduced by the comment "now I can tell you, this is
what I saw when my dead eye went wild" (40).[7]

In the embedded tale, a group of old men on a store porch in Louisiana
see a beautiful girl and lament, "There is a bad God," because their own
"old charade," their life story, which includes nothing like Celeste, is "rid-
dled with holes" (41). The narrator's own story offers a possible preclosure
point at which he first says that he has been "sober ever since" seeing Celeste and then immediately admits, "I have just told a lie" (42). Emphasizing the instability of this narrator is the fact that he does not "loiter" for
long at this juncture in the narrative; rather, he adds another "ending" in
which he at first claims, "At forty, I am at a certain peace" with love, money,
and a "closeness with my children . . . each . . . [one of which is] a hero bet-

7. "Ride, Fly, Penetrate, Loiter" was first published in *Georgia Review,* XXXVII (1983),
33–38. In "Iron Pony in the Ozarks," for *Condé Nast Traveler* (April, 1992), 162–67+, Hannah described a bike tour in which he and friends "set out to do the Ozarks on a 1987 Harley
Electra Glide Classic."

ter than yours" (42). In the final scene, however, he is not enjoying family "closeness." Rather, he is "light[ing] out for the Territory" again, "riding right into your face" across the country on his Triumph (43). As at the end of "Even Greenland," we are "looking at [the Hannah protagonist's] damned triumph" (*CM,* 34), with pun intended. In "Ride, Fly, Penetrate, Loiter," as in his fiction as a whole, Hannah's dizzying display of shifting story frames, together with his narrators' contradictory claims and disclaimers, contributes to the complexity of embedded layers of story beneath the bold, seemingly straightforward, "in your face" narrative surface.

"It Spoke of Exactly the Things" is another story in which the protagonist is a dreamer, a liar, a hater of frauds, such as his "last woman [who] couldn't even *appear* without a tribe of witnesses . . . [who with] her grown kids like[d] to sniff around beauty and grace, not touching it, like scared hyenas . . . [and] held to sanity so hard they were insane" (*CM,* 45). It is a satire on university life and thus an oblique commentary on those in Hannah's own profession. In the story, Ned has left a southern university because of academicians who are full of "nimble jabber," although they are "not worthy of shoveling Shakespeare's house of night soil" (46). As usual, the frustration with "every inconsequential fool who'd had his way with drying up the day" has driven this Hannah "hero" to "get drunk and fire at will" (46). The narrator-protagonist believes that a certain wildness is necessary to combat life's banality. The story is also a satire on Ned's new location and its obsession with health: California, "an excellent place for polishing your hatreds . . . [because] it requires high health to murder the day with banality" (47). The satire is ambivalent, however, because of Ned's fascination with heroes and thus with California's windsurfers, whose sport seems "a noble thing, with the danger required" (46).

The plot abruptly shifts to tell the story of a beautiful woman with a black butterfly tattooed between her breasts, who is constantly in the company of her "simpering pig" of a son (48), at one point presented in a mock-pietà scene. His hatred of the boy, "the gigolo of his mother's blind affection" (48), makes Ned decide to spray the offending son with "whaleshit . . . [which] they sell . . . for fertilizer" (47); and he does. But in spite of what Ned sees as an unnatural (Oedipal) relationship between mother and son, the woman's tattoo "spoke of exactly the things" he needs and desires: "It gave hope" (49). After rescuing the woman from this boy, he shifts into a wild tale in which an imagined lecture castigating a "swooning" academic audience is conflated with a sexual fantasy involving drugs, on a ship assailed by a storm with "a lightning run of astonishing proportions" (52). There are two major keys to this story—one symbolic and thematic, the other autobiographical. In the original story, published separately in a limited edition by Palaemon Press in 1982, the title was *Black Butterfly*. The "It" of the present title, "It Spoke of Exactly the Things," refers to the black butterfly as symbolic of the character's hope for some kind of life renewal, since the butterfly has long been a Christian symbol for resurrection. The autobiographical underpinnings of the story relate to a time when Hannah, by his own account, went into a California rehabilitation center for substance abuse—for "drying out." At a preclosure point in the story in which the narrator fantasizes sex as he stands "spreadlegged on deck" with the beautiful woman on her knees before him, "the black butterfly pumping between her breasts," he seems to signal conclusion with the ostensibly optimistic statement, "Bold as love, bold as love!" (52–53). The scene parodies those from the romantic swashbuckling movie adventures of Errol Flynn. However, a final, anticlimactic scene is rendered in images evoking Eliot's *Waste Land*. At this later time, Ned is apparently a beached derelict in a place "where the water washes in full of the rust from old wrecks, the rust from my sunken shotgun washing over her tanned feet, [from which position he says,] I sit, still stunned by carnivorous passion when the drug runs out" (53). The woman is still there but gone is the mock-heroic tone, as well as the pretense that "bold . . . love" will effect a renewal. The actual closure, then, is a sobering scene in which a substance abuser, incarcerated in his own addiction, admits, "I drank enough. I banged the walls of space and time long enough. I don't have to lie. I think of the black butterfly and sometimes I can even remember her name" (53).

What is real here? Perhaps, as in Hawthorne's short stories, several of which involve butterflies and the ideal of perfect love, the question of reality itself is an issue. Did Young Goodman Brown really go to a meeting of witches in the forest, or did he dream it? Did Hannah's protagonist really have any of these adventures, or are they alternate scenarios of a substance abuser's world, in which hallucination is the reality? In the American romance, and especially in the postmodern world, one cannot be certain. Postmodernists accept such uncertainty in both life and story; as one of postmodernism's premier writers, Thomas Pynchon, comments about his novel *V,* "Why should things be easy to understand?" Perhaps it is not beside the point that Pynchon, a writer of "difficult" novels is, in one of his worlds, a writer of liner notes for albums by Generation X rock-and-roll bands; like Hannah, a lover of rock and roll, Pynchon calls it "one of the last honorable callings."[8]

Hannah's fiction is never "easy," partly because its generic identity often ranges between allegory and parody. In "Getting Ready," also from *Captain Maximus,* Roger Laird is forty-eight years old and has "been everywhere after the big one, the lunker, the fish bigger than he was" (3). He is presented as something of a dandy, perhaps a Prufrock, since he "caught a crab . . . that reminded him of himself" (7). Roger, who has "an intelligent cranium, nicely shaped like that of a tamed, professional fisherman" (5), wades out into the surf and affects the stance of "a taller Napoléon surveying an opposing infantry horde from an unexpected country of idiots" (9). Furthermore, he has done research on the sport of fishing by watching television, by looking at adventure magazines while doing housework, and by having "read Izaak Walton . . . [although] he had no use for England and all that olden shit" (5).[9] When he finally hooks a sand shark "about four feet long and fifteen pounds," Roger is "yanked into the sea . . . floundering"; yet he manages to reel it in, "and it was *his*" (14). Needing help to unhook the little shark and refusing to allow another fisherman to kill it, Roger throws it back into the sea. It seems a trivial incident, but the event changes his life, first filling "his chest full of such good air it was like a gas of silver in him . . . [and] he did not know what kind of story to tell" (15); then, although bankrupt, he seems happier and his marriage is better.

This "fish story" closes with his walking through a lake on "stilts eight feet high . . . [that] made him stand twelve feet in the air," yelling at rich people in their boats "Fuck you! Fuck you!" (16). The ending seems ambiguous until one does the arithmetic: that Roger is only four feet tall—the same measure as the fish's length—suggests that he has completely identified with the creature. Looking back, one realizes that early on Roger has

8. Thomas Pynchon, quoted in Sharon Tregaskis, "Pynchon's Cool," *Cornell Magazine* (September, 1996), 104.

9. He refers to Izaak Walton's *The Compleat Angler,* published in the seventeenth century and still popular.

almost been pulled into the ocean by a big fish, which someone else has had to land for him, and that he describes the sand shark in terms similar to those he might use to describe himself: it is "a fish so young, so handsome, so perfect for its business, and [yet] so unlucky" (14), because it is, like Roger, "floundering" after being "yanked" around by rich people. Also related to Roger's identity crisis is the otherwise vague passage about the rich man, Mr. Mintner, whom Roger "believed . . . should be hauled away and made to eat with accountants" (8), in other words, with the kind of sinners represented in the Bible by the tax collectors with whom Jesus condescended to share a meal. The image of Roger on stilts in the lake, which constitutes a parody of Jesus walking on the water, also provides context for Roger's "Jesus—oh, thank you" comment (14) and links the story with biblical parables of rich men, sinners, and big fish stories, as well as with the early Christian fish symbol, thus with the martyrdom of Jesus, and apparently with Roger's image of himself as a victim and martyr. Especially because Roger has more control over the life of his fish alter ego than he has had over his own life, setting it free has a salutary effect on his attitude toward life.

For a four-foot-tall man like Roger, a four-foot fish is a huge catch. As in "Getting Ready," in "Idaho," the narrator-protagonist, a writer, is eager to identify with "an immense something," specifically Richard Hugo, an important poet associated with the story's setting in the "big sky" country of Montana (*CM,* 17). This protagonist is also a mediocre man suffering from hero worship, wondering, "Where are you giants anymore?" (20). He has "hope for the big thing" and is "greedy for the miracle" (22), and he wants an Idaho patch for his jacket, perhaps because Ernest Hemingway, another "giant," loved the state. Despite the pervasive allusions to both popular romantic and modernist existential hero stories, especially to Hemingway-esque "big fish" stories, Hannah is after different "fish." That the Hannah protagonist is the postmodern, hero manqué counterpart of Hemingway and his characters is confirmed not only by their radical shifts from one narrative tone to another throughout their stories but also by the linguistic excess that suggests their playful, even joyful, defiance of the worst indignities of human existence.

The sports-hero motif is continued in "Fans," where football is the sport. Wright, the narrator whose name signals his craft, is the son of an alcoholic described as a "sportswriter and a hack and a shill for the university team" (*CM,* 55). Young Wright, like Hannah, had apparently been too small to play football in high school and instead became a poet and a musician in the band. The setting of "Fans" is a bar in Oxford, Mississippi, home of fierce traditional college football rivalries. It is "the morning of the big game . . . [a] bright wonderful football morning pouring in with the green trees, the Greek-front buildings, and the yelling frat boys" (55). Inside the bar, however, are four symbolically limited, unheroic men. There is Wright himself, who has a "condition" (59) that we come to understand is mental and that may be due to a lifetime of abuse. In addition, there is his alcoholic father "Milton, who was actually blind but nevertheless a rabid fan" (55), and Loomis Orange, a character who is "an ugly, distorted little toad," perhaps meant to parody Carson McCullers' hunchbacked homosexual dwarf, Cousin Lyman, who suffers from unrequited love in *The Ballad of the Sad Café* (56).

Readers familiar with Hannah's Civil War stories will notice that the football hero of "Fans," J. Edward Toole, or J. E. T., has had his nickname shortened to simply "Jet," in the same fashion that Confederate general J. E. B. Stuart's became "Jeb." Wright, eager to identify with the star player, who "was always large and swift," begins to reminisce about their high school years. The alcoholic father tries to stop him, but Wright launches into a romanticized story of Jet. "I know him well," he says. "We were little strangers on this earth together. We gamboled in the young pastures. We took our first forbidden pleasures together . . . I shared my poetry with him" (57). The father knows what is coming but is powerless to prevent Wright's telling of what are, against all reason, treasured memories of how Jet repeatedly humiliated him: by shooting him with air rifles, by turning his poems into pornography, and by "clotheslining" him on his new motor scooter after graduation. At last, he tells of Jet's pushing him into shark-infested waters where someone had been feeding the sharks razor blades wrapped in hamburger meat until the water was "a fan of blood" (60). The metaphor constitutes a pun that identifies Wright, himself a "fan of blood," with the victimized sharks; for like the sharks, dumb beasts that they are, Wright has kept coming back for more punishment, as if he were eating razor blades in a blind feeding frenzy of hero worship. The fish as alter ego, of course, constitutes an intertextual link to "Getting Ready," as well as to other stories with split protagonists as "interesting monsters."

Like any good storyteller, Wright adds suspense before his grand finale. "Then," he begins, pausing dramatically; Loomis, leaning forward in anticipation repeats, "*Then?*"; and the elder Wright, who realizes that he does not yet know the worst, demands, "*Then? Then?*" (59). The final "beautiful thing" Wright remembers is that a year after the incident, and after Jet had won a Sugar Bowl game and become a "born again" Christian, he had apologized to Wright. Had the story ended there, we might think of it as the story of Jet and Wright. But one paragraph remains, in which the four men leave for the stadium "to wait for Jet to kill [the opposing football team]" (60). Only then, perhaps, does it become clear that the distortion that has made these characters "grotesques" is their love of violence. It is as much their story as it is the story of the two younger men; thus, the title implies that they are all fans of blood.

Violence to the self, even acts that result in self-annihilation, are not too extreme for some of Hannah's characters, who refuse to be satiated by ordinary means. In "Even Greenland," the narrator, a writer and a jet pilot, is involved with his copilot, John, in an ongoing rivalry over who can have the most original experience. Complaining that nothing "much matters after you've seen the curvature of the earth" (*CM,* 31), he says that "even Greenland . . . [is] not fresh . . . [because] there are footsteps in the snow" (32). The narrator, attempting to show that he understands, draws an analogy with the feeling he had as a child in Mississippi, when he could be "the first up and there's been nobody in the snow, no footsteps" (32); but his very telling about it upsets John, who did not get to tell the story first. He apparently feels like a writer who sees what he thought was an original story published first by someone else: "You son of a bitch, that was *mine*—that snow in Mississippi. Now it's all shot to shit" (33). The only unique act that seems to remain for John is to go down with his plane. He insists that his friend eject while he flies straight up, not "seeking the earth at all," and demanding, "Just let me have *that* one, will you?" (33). Hannah's concern here not only with monstrous originality in terms of distortion of personality but also with prodigious writing is apparent from the otherwise incongruous emphasis on the tools of the writer's trade in the midst of the suicidal crisis. When John flies so fast that the wings catch fire, "the paper from his kneepad was flying all over the cockpit, and [the narrator] could see [John's] hand flapping up and down with the pencil in it, angry" (33). What might have seemed a random image early on in the story is revealed as significant when one remembers that these characters are, for Hannah, primarily two competing storytellers. John had wanted to make up for some "bad writing" by creating a story that would metaphorically "smoke" his friend (31); ironically, however, he can accomplish this only by literally "smoking" himself: by killing himself in a fiery—but original—crash. The narrator knows, later as he and his girlfriend Celeste "look at the burn," that he is "looking at John's damned triumph" (34).

The most important "monsters" in Hannah's stories are military and sports heroes, writers and storytellers, musicians and other artist characters, all of whom are in some sense aspects of Hannah the storyteller, the creative artist. For many years, as he admits, Hannah worked at creating himself in the persona of an "interesting monster"; yet he is concerned less with his autobiography for its own sake than with the story itself, including the omnipresent substory of the writer at work and of the writing process. And even in this complex and discontinuous fiction, the story he is telling is the story of ordinary life, which itself is broken into various levels of reality; for the form of Hannah's fiction reflects what Thomas Pavel calls a culture's "ontological landscape," which commonly shifts from one reality to another: from our ordinary working world to escapes into such "leisure ontologies" as movies, fiction, computer games, sex, drugs, and other "mental management of routine"—alternate modes of being. Thus, concludes Brian McHale, "Postmodernist fiction *does* hold the mirror up to reality; but that reality, now more than ever before, is plural."[10]

Basic to all of Hannah's fiction and consonant with its emphasis on the debunking of illusions is the theme of truth versus falsehood, a variation on the classic theme of appearance versus reality, which for Hannah is often a metaphor for the relation of art to life. Serving as a sort of coda for this theme are the lead stories in two collections, "Water Liars" in *Airships* and "High-Water Railers" in *Bats Out of Hell,* both of which derive from an

---

10. Pavel, quoted in McHale, *Postmodernist Fiction,* 36–37; McHale, *Ibid.,* 39, emphasis McHale's.

even earlier story, "All the Old Harkening Faces at the Rail." These stories are connected not only by some common characters with common concerns; they also move toward similar crises, each of which involves a woman whose presence forces some truth upon a group of men whose lies and denials have been their only bulwark against humiliation and the resulting outrage in the face of their failure to live up to cultural myths about male identity and their failure to recognize or admit some truths about female identity. The "big fish" stories and other lies, mainly about sex, which form the verbal competition of the middle-aged "water liars" in the early story, are followed by something of a conventional epiphany, when the narrator and the old storyteller realize that they are "kindred" because they both have been "crucified by the truth" (*A*, 7). In "High-Water Railers," however, similar talk is followed not by an epiphany but by a series of confessions that are mere extensions of their bragging.[11]

In "High-Water Railers," ninety-one-year-old Lewis, one of the "railers," describes his confessions as "sins of omission": those he has "omitted to *sin*" (*BOH*, 3). When Melanie, the widow of a former member of the group of aged liars, arrives on the symbolically shaking pier that has long been their meeting place, her motive is apparently to explain the scandal of her deceased husband's suddenly turning homosexual near the end of his life; by her candor, she effectively shows the men how to be true to themselves. Lewis begins to cry "like a child," allowing himself the tears he has never shed for the dog he has never admitted wanting. The story ends as they all start for Vicksburg in search of a dog, with "Melanie indicating the way" (11). Thus, the erstwhile "confessions," which may have seemed to counter the earlier lies in each story, are shown to be specious by a relative outsider, a catalytic figure who injects a note of reality. In "High-Water Railers," then, the extra "beat" that Melanie adds to the railers' self-pitying refrain alters the narrative rhythm, providing not closure but a new openness in the story and, it is implied, in the characters' individual stories.

Close readers of Hannah will notice that his fiction is both structurally and thematically of a piece, regardless of its wide variety of surface narratives. An example is seen in the structure of "Water Liars," in which the

11. Barry Hannah, "All the Old Harkening Faces at the Rail," *Fiction*, V (1978), 132–35.

narrative more closely fits the profile of an epiphanic story than does "High-Water Railers"; its preclosure epiphany, however, is upstaged by one final plot twist. Had "Water Liars" ended when the "older guy with a big hurting bosom" is forced to recognize the truth of his daughter's sexuality, it would have been a different story. As it stands, a second epiphany closes the frame tale and redirects attention from the father's pain to the narrator's relation to the old liar: they are "kindred." The shift to the more general perspective of men betrayed, in this case by a reality that denies the genteel southern notion of what a man's daughter is like, modifies the plot structure with the added narrative "beat" and thus aligns the story with the debunking technique, even though epiphanies are present. The "interesting monster" in this story, although rumored to be a ghost that the men think they hear in the woods, is actually the truthteller himself, whose true story frightens them and perhaps will haunt them, as a ghost might—and as the truths of Hannah's fiction might haunt his readers.

Even if the lead story in *Bats Out of Hell* were not a sort of sequel to "Water Liars," it, like all of the stories in *Bats Out of Hell*, would seem familiar to readers because of Hannah's signature linguistic brilliance, his grim comedy, and his obsession with sex, violence, and heroes. Other new stories in the collection, however, are like the new poems of Newt Ross in "Hey, Have You Got a Cig, the Time, the News, My Face?": they are "extraordinary, going places glad and hellish he'd never approached before" (*BOH*, 336). Many of these stories are marked not only by a lack of formal unity but also by an exaggerated self-reflexivity. During his radio interview with Tom Vitale, Hannah said that he felt more "with the human struggle" in writing this book; in addition, it is apparent that he is never out of sight of the particular struggle of the writer. For where Hannah goes in *Bats Out of Hell* is into the self-conscious presence of the writer and the oral storyteller at work, into the skeletal structure of the story and into the great reservoir of styles and genres that are mixed in this book with joyous abandon, perhaps surpassed only by such intertextuality as is found in Laurence Sterne's *Tristram Shandy* and James Joyce's *Ulysses* and *Finnegans Wake*. In spite of the condensed, elliptical nature of Hannah's often cryptic prose, throughout the book Hannah's narrators take the time to address the reader directly, sometimes in the mode of a nineteenth-century romance. The topic of these self-reflexive comments is often the act of writing itself. In

"The Spy of Loog Root," for example, the narrator confides, "Reader, not often do we discover the grand old monologues in us, in our noisy crowded age, where conversation, especially out here [in the West] comes down nearly to 'yup' and 'nope'" (*BOH,* 142). About frontier justice, this teller remarks, "Much of that is done in the wilds of Montana, let me caution the reader" (145).

The self-reflexive quality of Hannah's fiction is also demonstrated in the title story, "Bats Out of Hell Division," in which the struggle of writing per se is as important a subject as is the fictional Civil War battle recounted in the plot. The soldier-scribe's narration is worth quoting at length, since it illustrates several aspects of the story's self-reflexiveness. He begins by explaining the name of his military division in the Confederate Army:

> We, *in a ragged bold line across their eyes, come on.* Shreds of the flag leap back from the pole held by Billy, then Ira. We, you'd suspect, my posteritites, are not getting on too well. They have shot hell out of us. More properly we are merely the Bats by now. Our cause is leaking, the fragments of it left around those great burned holes, as if their general put his cigar *into the document* a few times. . . . . But we're still out there. We gain by inches, then lose by yards. But back by inches over the night. . . . Something about us their cannon doesn't like, to put it mildly. By now you must know that half our guns are no good, either.
>
> Estes—as I spy around—gets on without buttocks, just hewn off one sorry cowardly night. . . . I have become the *scribe*—not voluntarily, but because all limbs are gone except *my writing arm.* (*BOH,* 43; emphasis added)

The subtext of writing and the writer, emphasized in the passage above, which debunks the illusion of the story as mimesis in the traditional sense (that is, in Erich Auerbach's sense of mimesis—literature as mirror of life) and the illusion of writing as carefully ordered, is here made plain. Close under the surface of the surreal war story is the story of what writers have always known about literary creation: that from "a ragged bold line [of print or script] across our eyes," we, the writers, "come on," telling and re-telling; that often "our cause is leaking, the fragments of it left around . . . great burned holes . . . [; and that yet] we're still out there [writing]. We gain by inches, then lose by yards. But back by inches over the night." The subtext embedded in the narrative depicts the writing process as a disorderly struggle—as, in fact, a battle—that may seem as if it, like the presence of Emmaline, the "benign crone of a nurse," is "part of no plan at all" (43) but is rather a series of desperate measures that press into service any likely "writing arm." From there, it is only a short step to the borrowing from other literary "arms," which, of course all writers do.

Hannah's literary borrowing is sometimes oblique and subtle, sometimes transparent. In "Bats," both the words and meter of the clause "Something about us their cannon doesn't like" echo a line from Robert Frost's "Mending Wall": "Something there is that doesn't love a wall." Such evidence of Hannah's consciousness of rhythm pervades his fiction, constantly reminding the reader of his musicality and emphasizing the fact that he is a poet of time, not space. Intertextual borrowing is also suggested by Hannah's "the foul hospital" of the Civil War (*BOH*, 43), which seems to echo William Carlos Williams' "contagious hospital" from "Spring and All." In "The Spy of Loog Root," both the narrator's "need" [of] the sense . . . that [he is] watched" (150) and his branding of a voyeuristic young writer as a "thief . . . stealing all my time" (139), are clear links, as we have seen, not only to the postmodern style and unreliable narrator of *Pale Fire* but also to *Timon of Athens,* to which Nabokov's title alludes, and to the "thief of time" theme in both.

Both self-reflexivity and intertextual borrowing are also integral to "Evening of the Yarp: A Report by Roonswent Dover," in which the narrator begins, "Darn it were boring, wisht I were a hawk or crab" (*BOH*, 91). Immediately, then, and as magically as the young Arthur in T. H. White's *The Once and Future King* was changed by the sorcerer Merlin into a falcon, then a fish, the writer-character in Hannah's tale is transformed into an oral storyteller who spins a yarn worthy of the oldest Ozark folktale. Moreover, this storyteller persona doubles as a character that is perhaps dear to the heart of Hannah the teacher of creative writing: Roonswent Dover is a gifted but almost illiterate writer. The urgency of the artist's vision can be heard in Roonswent's disclaimer: "Deacon Charles at the VT school say go a head and write like this dont change. He wants to see it quick cause I seen the Yarp. Or somebody like him. Xcuse me please for not correct but I am hard attempting to spell at least sweller it being so important" (91). The suggestion is that Deacon Charles has recognized a writer with a true vision that must be transcribed while it is fresh and before it is lost: Roonswent has "seen the Yarp." Moreover, Hannah's Arkansas hill-country storyteller appeals not only to the American myth of the innocent Adam but also to an ancient Hebrew narrative tradition, in the legendary Yarp's Samson-like complaint that he has "been womaned." As a result, says the supernatural "interesting monster" of Roonswent's tale, "I aint half the Yarp . . . I used to be" (101). Since the Yarp, one of Hannah's strangest monsters, is a storyteller, too, it is appropriate that his name conflates two terms for narrative: the "yarn" of the oral storytelling tradition and the "barbaric yawp," as Walt Whitman called his epic poem "Song of Myself."

Ironically, the Yarp, who hitches a ride down the mountain in Roonswent's truck, berates the nineteen-year-old for the natives' habit of "legending" (93). "You know too many legends, boy. Everybody does. You got to lie to stay halfway interested in yourself, dont you? The imagination is what ruins it. They shouldn't never imagined heaven nor hell" (93). When the boy objects, claiming that he "just fix[es] small engines," the Yarp retorts, "You lie!" (93). The exclamation speaks to several levels of text and subtext in the story. Because of the Yarp's previous identity of the lie with the act of the imagination in "legending," the comment acts as a pun on creating legends and lying about it. Because the Yarp is also a storyteller, his lament about the creation of legends is a self-contradiction that debunks the unity of the story. Moreover, the Yarp's charge—"You got to lie to stay halfway interested in yourself"—constitutes an intertextual reference within the Hannah canon that connects Roonswent with Hannah's many other narrator-liars, who, like the young protagonist in *Boomerang*, want to "make something happen in vacant air [that is] a sweet revenge on reality" (*B*, 17).

In no other story of *Bats Out of Hell* is Hannah's writer persona more central or more transparent, or the artist-creator less a distant Joycean divinity sitting aloof, than in "The Spy of Loog Root"; here the narrator reveals, "I went about my days, speaking dialogues . . . [and] acting old and new thoughts out, while the microscopic men, women and babies fought it out inside me for my soul" (*BOH*, 150). The plight of the writer is also shown in the kind of Nabokovian images of mirrorlike reflections that are integral to *Pale Fire;* in the voyeurism of the adolescent writer who watches people carefully through a telescope, "showing his prurient interest in civilization" (132); and in the self-reflexivity of the narrator, self-named as "your good village philosopher" (140), who, through the telescope, watches the writer "hoarding his visions and dialogues" (133). On one narrative level, the storyteller persona subtly merges with the alienated self that, on another level, is in an identity crisis, when the narrator's own "cursing and whimper[ing]" causes him to see the boy as "another version of myself beside me" (136). Stories that are informed by the oral storytelling tradition, such as "The Spy of Loog Root" and "Evening of the Yarp," provide another strong link to the generally experimental nature of the short story and to the nonlinear nature of most American fiction, since the novel too has been so clearly influenced by the orality of the short-story genre and by its "retention of such older narrative traditions as parables, animal fables, and fairy tales," as Mary Louise Pratt argues in distinguishing between traits of the short story and the novel.[12]

In "Two Things, Dimly, Were Going at Each Other," Hannah's writer-character is Coots, who some call a "profane dope fiend and pederast who wrote gibberish" (*BOH,* 29). Coots is also the alter-ego of an "old coot," Dr. Latouche, whose story Coots tells. In Coots's "manly midwestern prose," we are told that "many, hordes, died" (15–16). Coots discusses his notes for a "space-time narrative" about the West in terms of "common threads of magic in random clippings from various sources" (29). Because of Hannah's repeated references to the writing process, he, like Eudora Welty, another Mississippi writer of lyric, antimimetic short stories, is always writing about writing. One of the "common threads of magic" in Hannah's fiction is the recurrence of internal mirror images that show forth the fractal quality of a work or of his complete works: in other words, individual events serve as fractals that mirror the whole on a small scale. In this story, Hannah's narrator creates a new folktale based on a weird, legendary creature called "the grofft," said to inhabit Central America, and whose bite causes "doglike barking and whining, quadriped posture, hebephrenia; extremely nervous devotion to a search, general agitation, constant disappointment; lethargy, then renewal" (21). This monster's behavior is remarkably like that of Hannah's antiheroic characters, who sulk about nervously and talk to themselves, who are often agitated and often, if illogically, renewed. The

12. Mary Louise Pratt, "The Short Story: The Long and the Short of It," *Poetics,* X (1981), 180, 187.

monster as alter ego of the protagonist, then, is a narrative strategy that in effect asks ontological questions about which self is real. Coots is entranced by old Dr. Latouche, who has contracted the grofft disease, the symptoms of which are activated by some "imagery" on the writer's wall. Latouche runs, maddened, into the night to his death. The self-reflexive story ends as Coots bemoans the end of Harry Latouche, the protagonist in his grofft story: "But what a gap, Harry," Coots laments over Harry's corpse. "What an awful gap you leave. And I only a watcher" (39). Hannah's language here suggests the emptiness a writer may feel when the story is done; the final image of the writer who is "only a watcher" in the night constitutes an intertextual reference to Hannah's own novel *Nightwatchmen* and to his many other stories featuring voyeur characters. Interestingly, the theme of the alienated watcher is important to other southern writers, including Walker Percy and, most recently, Richard Ford. In Ford's *Independence Day,* the themes of watching and of rage result from his characters' feelings of wariness, helplessness, and general anxiety. His protagonist, Frank Bascombe, who struggles with commitment to fatherhood and a new love relationship after a failed marriage, often drives through sleeping towns late at night "to take a *look* but not to touch or feel or be involved . . . [because] there is sovereign civic good in being a bystander, a watcher." Hannah's "Two Things, Dimly," in which Coots is both the "watcher" and alter ego of his own character, Harry Latouche, presents a paradox of characterization that contributes to Hannah's debunking of the illusion of an integrated self.[13]

In the oblique story that Coots narrates as a Western, made of "common threads of magic in random clippings from various sources," some intertextual references seem almost "throwaway" comments, yet they add to the texture of a fiction that consistently conflates art and life. For example, when Coots refers to the "superb . . . air [that] might give him a few more years, a few more books" in the Lawrence, Kansas, setting of his work in progress, he calls Lawrence "the scratchy, potent West" (*BOH,* 29), alluding to Stephen Crane's "The Bride Comes to Yellow Sky." In Crane's story, Scratchy, who wants to continue living a fiction about a "potent West" of perpetual gunfights, must face the unromantic fact that his dueling partner

13. Richard Ford, *Independence Day* (New York, 1995), 424; emphasis Ford's.

has ended their imaginary boylife together by getting married. (Similarly, in Hannah's "Scandal d'Estime," Harold's search for a magnificent, self-defining scandal is also aborted by marriage, a fate successfully avoided by innocent American Adams since Fenimore Cooper's Natty Bumppo, alias Hawkeye, *et al.,* of the Leatherstocking Tales.) Intertextual links within Hannah's works are exemplified by the Crane allusion in "Two Things, Dimly," which in turn shares similar subject matter and narrative techniques with *Never Die,* a novel both intertextual and transgeneric that is Hannah's most extensive tribute to the romance of the American West. In the opening paragraph of *Never Die,* we encounter twelve-year-old Kyle Nitburg in the fairytale formula of a boy who lives in New Orleans with his "poor but beautiful" mother; by the second page, Nitburg has moved west and married Nancy Beech, "from an old distinguished but poor family" (1–2). Between these two pages, however, is an oblique inversion of the Hansel and Gretel plot, in which the poor but kind woodcutter marries the wicked stepmother, who turns out two innocent children, to let them starve in the forest. In Hannah's novel, the young but wicked Kyle turns in his mother to the Union forces as a spy and reaps a reward of "one hundred real dollars" as she is hanged; later, when the adult Kyle tires of his wife, he sells her into slavery to a Comanche chief for "four thousand dollars in real gold" (1–2). Clearly, this narrative announces itself as a freewheeling multiple parody of many genres, including the fairytale, the sentimental romance, the Western, and the tall tale (see Chapter 4).

Narratives that are characterized by unsettling shifts, gaps, and disavowals of their own truth are in the tradition of some of the finest American works of literature, those which, Richard Chase argues, "achieve their very being, their energy and form, from the perception and acceptance not of unities but of radical disunities."[14] In many Hannah stories, such shifts are much more unsettling than the shift in perspective at the end of "Water Liars." For a person reading Hannah in the order of publication, even the astonishing stories of *Airships* might not provide proper warning for *Ray,* a novella that careens from one perspective to another, one war to another, one century to another. The entire content of Chapter 5 is this: "I live in so

---

14. Richard Chase, *The American Novel and Its Tradition* (Garden City, N.Y., 1957), 6–7.

many centuries. Everybody is still alive" (*R,* 41). Yet Ray, the narrator-protagonist, speaking of himself in the third person, seems at home in this psychic chaos, asserting that "without a healthy sense of confusion, Ray might grow smug" (103). Of course, since all of Hannah's protagonists are liars, and since Ray is as often distraught as he is smug, this character fails to convince us that his confusion is healthy. Ray is a physician and a former pilot who served in Vietnam; the opening chapter, however, reveals that he is also a patient—an alcoholic—who introduces himself *to* himself by naming things peripheral to himself:

> Ray, you are a doctor and you are in a hospital in Mobile, except now you are a patient but you're still me. Say what? You say you want to know who I am?
> I have a boat on the water. I have magnificent children. I have a wife who turns her beauty on and off like a light switch. (3)

One kind of hybrid "monster" in Hannah's fiction is the character who sometimes describes himself in terms of airplanes, sex, and weapons. Describing the experience of piloting a Lear jet while he exhorts himself to emerge from the depression for which he is hospitalized, Ray exclaims, "You can do it, mind and heart. You can give it the throttle and pick up your tail and ease it on" (4). Ray often conflates not only the wars but also the individual images, resulting in centaurlike metaphors, reification of characters, or personifications of weapons as sexual objects. "Oh, help me!" he begins Chapter 10, "I am losing myself in two centuries and two wars. The SAM missile came up, the heat-seeker. It stood up in front of me like a dick at twenty thousand feet" (45). After describing how he saved the life of his friend Quisenberry by strafing the beach in his F-4 Phantom jet, he says, "I am very proud of the things I did for my country. I fought for the trees, the women, who, when they quit talking, will let you, etc. . . . Whoever created Ray gave him a big sex engine" (46; ellipsis Hannah's). Agonizing over his marriage woes, he complains,

> Ray is crawling this afternoon. Many things have broken down in our nice house. The only glory I see is the glory I saw as a jet fighter. I went through the clouds and brought up the nose of the Phantom, lifting at twenty-one hundred land miles per hour. It was either them or me, by God. I loved those

clean choices. And I loved my jet. I loved all those aerodynamics, the rising
and diving.

Something's wrong.

Westy and I are not close in the old way. (101–102)

The two ostensibly separate subjects in this passage are actually related in
the same way as are two images in a haiku, which are also presented without transition. The implied comparison is between the masculine world of
war and the ostensibly more feminized world of marriage. In marriage,
one's world is not made of the "clean choices" available to the wartime pilot, for whom it was "either them or me." In one of the passages in which
Ray imagines himself a Confederate cavalryman, the general gives the order "Raise sabers!" and Ray's responding comment reifies all men: "Eventually every man's a sword" (108). Hannah complicates all such images of
the phallic in several ways. On the most basic level, as expressed in Ray's
fantasies that approximate what Jayne Anne Phillips calls "machine
dreams" (in her novel of that name), they constitute the clichéd metaphor
of the (positive masculine) penetrating phallus; on the intermediate level,
they signify the (ambiguous male-female) sexual relationship in marriage;
and at the opposite extreme, they suggest the (negative masculine) metaphor of the Confederate saber, a symbol of defeat. Even the "positive masculine" image, as Owen Gilman, Jr., has explained, has long been compro-
mised in the American mind by the "conflation of male action in war and
sex," in other words, with the kind of phallic violence that Hannah protagonists such as Ray promote as positive.[15]

Ray, the form of which is so startlingly different from his first two novels,
is the first of Hannah's books that clearly announces him as a postmodernist. In this short novel he employs an extremely fragmented narrative and
an unstable field of wordplay, both of which on the surface resemble Faulkner's experimental modernism in the narrative structure of *As I Lay Dying,*
including unusual perspective and several one- and two-sentence chapters.
However, Hannah's technique, which includes multiple perspectives
within one character, more closely resembles surfiction, the mode often
identified as postmodern or postcontemporary, which Raymond Federman

15. Jayne Anne Phillips, *Machine Dreams* (New York, 1984); Gilman, *Vietnam and the
Southern Imagination,* 88–89.

defines in terms of fiction that is experimental to the point of radical rebellion against traditional forms, a fiction "that reveals man's irrationality rather than man's rationality." Ronald Sukenick, another postcontemporary literary theorist, defines surfiction as disruptive and subversive, its form "an object of invention . . . [and] a dynamic rather than an inert element of composition."[16]

Even the surface narrative of *Ray* consists of two levels: it is the story of Ray and his relation to the Hooch family, especially to Sister, who is a "violent [sexual] delight" (47), and to her father, a morphine addict and poet; it is also the story of Ray's second marriage. Strangely, his relationship with the Hooches seems to mean more to Ray than does his wife Westy, to whom he is continually unfaithful with Sister and others. Especially his connection with Mr. Hooch, a surrogate father manqué, seems to afford some kind of reciprocal nurturing-healing benefit. Interrupting the narrative macrostructure of desire, despair, and hope in *Ray* are a long digression into the history of Hernando de Soto, who may be the ancestor of a minor character in the book; a series of flashbacks from Ray's service as a Navy pilot in Vietnam; several fantasies based on the Civil War; scenes in a hospital emergency room, including detailed medical procedures and prescriptions; poems; sketches of various other escapades involving sex and/or violence; and a tribute to Ray's stepson—all in one hundred and thirteen pages. Michael P. Spikes suggests that the narrative contradictions and discontinuities in the novel are countered by the "unifying and centering Will" of the narrator, because Ray constantly objectifies himself: in his third-person references to himself, his name is a "stable unit of meaning" or a "rigid designator." Spikes also points to Ray's repeated comments about his own narration, a "representational form" through which he consciously creates a self in a "will toward stability." However, this constant need for repetition seems to emphasize the constant struggle of a self calling out in crisis, as if Ray is trying to reassure himself that he exists. It also foregrounds the writer's struggle to create meaning out of the chaos of life through the "representational form" of art. Ray's life, then, represents art.[17]

One of the greatest contradictions in *Ray* is the protagonist's vacillation

16. Federman, ed., *Surfiction,* 3; Ronald Sukenick, *In Form: Digressions on the Art of Fiction* (Carbondale, Ill., 1985), ix, 9–13.

17. Spikes, "What's in a Name?" 69, 78–82.

between despair and hope. At one point, in a morose meditation, itself full of inner contradictions, he declares, "Yes, I have seen the rain coming down on a sunny day. I have seen the moon hot and the sun cold. I have seen almost everything dependable go against its nature. I have seen needless death and I have seen needless life" (70). Yet, again and again, he fights against the despair, usually in terms of the Confederates of the Lost Cause who, despite every setback, charge the enemy, as he does at the end of Chapter 15, mixing metaphors of the Civil War and Vietnam:

> Christ, here we go. Not a chance, but what a territory to gain!
> Their cannon just missed me as my horse started running on the water. We are high on our horses and laughing and I can hear the shrill Rebel yell behind me. They are throwing out phosphorus bombs, and I see some of the men go down. My men just laugh and the horses climb the banks. What an open field. We are laughing and screaming the yell.
> It is an open field. (109)

The image of the raised sword recurs like a leitmotif throughout the book as a symbol of hope in the midst of despair, no matter what the crisis; for Owen Gilman, it is "that magical male saber, risen to again set wrongs right, ready at an impulse for the charge to glory."[18] With that image the book ends, along with references to a mixture of hopeful and lost causes:

> Ray, yes, Ray! Doctor Ray is okay!
> Charlie DeSoto and Eileen are together again. The nurses are getting married. Westy is coming with the hot oils and the balm. The Alabama team is still whipping everybody in sight. . . . Mr. Hooch has his hands on a pencil.
> Sister!
> Christians!
> Sabers, gentlemen, sabers! (113)

It is also not beside the point that the dust jackets of the last two Hannah books depict several "Screaming Rebel Rockets." In *Bats Out of Hell*, the firecrackers are pictured as if coming out of the mouth of a screaming panther; in *High Lonesome*, they are placed in an empty Coke bottle, a com-

---

18. Gilman, *Vietnam and the Southern Imagination*, 89.

mon launch vehicle of bottle rockets in the South, which here also suggests a pencil holder on a writer's desk and thus the "screaming Rebel rockets" that are Hannah's stories. ("Rebel" would always be capitalized in the diction of the traditional South.)

In the Twayne *Barry Hannah,* Charney focuses on the stories in *Captain Maximus,* which he identifies as surfiction, but much of Hannah's fiction is in some degree marked by surfictionist or other postmodernist traits. Despite his postmodern poetics, however, Hannah is at heart a romantic writer, a fact that is nowhere more clear than in his mingling of the ideas of beauty and death. For example, when describing Charlie DeSoto's obsession about killing Mr. Wently, Ray's mood suddenly shifts to the pastoral: "One day it was a glorious day, and the red and yellow leaves were falling all around the street, since it was fall, the dying beautiful season of the year" (*R,* 13). The description is reminiscent of both Poe's theory of poetic beauty and of Shelley's "Ode to the West Wind," but in Hannah the juxtaposition of pastoral images with those of urban and personal blight creates a dark irony.[19]

The combination of postmodernist technique and romantic sensibility results in a disjunction that is one of the most obvious aspects of creative organic disunity in Hannah's stories, and in their lack of formal unity they most clearly differ from modernist epiphanic stories. In "Scandale d'Estime," from *Bats Out of Hell,* the narrative shifts from first to second person, from one narratological time frame to another and from one shameful episode to another, as George, the seventeen-year-old narrator of the frame tale, and Harold, the protagonist of a story within the frame, seek to transform debilitating shame into empowering scandal; claims Harold, "Nobody throbs in shame, derided worldwide" (204). The title is a pun on the French expression "*succès d'estime,*" a term that is ordinarily applied to a novel or a play that is critically acclaimed but not popular with the general public. The term might well apply to the critically acclaimed fiction of Barry Hannah. But Hannah has modified this expression by substituting *scandale* for *succès.* In French, the word *scandale* suggests, first of all, the notion of sin in a religious sense, the primary example being Christ's crucifixion as *le scandale du monde,* and second, the related sins of those who cause

19. Charney, *Barry Hannah,* 70–83.

others to sin by turning from God and those who sin by inflicting injury upon innocents. "Scandal *pierces,* is *poignant, piquant, resonant,*" declares Harold, who, ironically, is seeking the "scandale d'estime," an elitist phenomenon that must be explained to the uninitiated (204). Thus, he explains to George: "Scandal is *delicious,* little man. All we are is obsession and pain. That is *all* humans are. And when these wild things go public, and are met with howls, they ring out the only honest history we have! They are *unbearable!* Magnificent! Wicked! . . . What they really are is raving on the heath, little man, in their honest unbearable humanity!" (204–205). The obvious allusion to Shakespeare's great tragedy links Hannah's version of the tragedy of every "little man" to that of King Lear, whose "raving on the heath" is a venerable symbol of "honest unbearable humanity." More recent British avatars of the archetype are Lord Byron's Manfred, Mary Shelley's monster in *Frankenstein,* and Emily Brontë's Heathcliff in *Wuthering Heights.* Ironically, perhaps, the link is every bit as strong to some American classics: Salinger's young narrator in *The Catcher in the Rye,* who declares that he is a "madman"; and Thomas Wolfe's protagonist in *Of Time and the River,* who describes himself as "so strong, so mad, so certain, and so lost [that he] hurls the great shoulder of his strength forever against phantasmal barriers."[20]

That the two-man dialogue and the similar theme in "Scandal d'Estime" parody the theatre of the absurd, and thus the similarity of life to art, is confirmed by the reference to an old man in the hotel lobby as "sitting the night in the same chair, full speed ahead with his tangled stare, a silent movie of *Godot,*" even "further gone into real life" (206). When Harold's search for scandal is cut short by marriage, the frame tale continues with George and his "pal" Horace, whom he constantly compares with Harold from the inner story. Another link between the two levels of narrative is a fictional character who George identifies only as New York Slim, whose story has been a two-year fantasy for him. As if a movie character has emerged from the screen and taken on flesh, New York Slim materializes as Felice. Part of George's fantasy has been to regard himself as a "Prince Val-

20. See *Le Petit Robert Dictionnaire de la Langue Française* (1976); Salinger, *Catcher in the Rye,* 1 *et passim;* Thomas Wolfe, *Of Time and the River* (1935; rpr. New York, 1944), quoted in Rubin, *The Mockingbird in the Gum Tree,* 99. For this reminder, I thank Professor Rubin, to whose matchless scholarship I am continually indebted.

iant" who can save his fictional maiden in distress, "forcing [him]self toward love of her [so that] even the muscle lines in her face would go away if
[he] loved her right" (210–11). In his depiction of George's adolescent fervor, Hannah pays homage to James Joyce through his echoing of "Araby."
Like Joyce's young protagonist, who adores Mangan's sister in a halo of light
"at the railings," entranced by "the white border of a petticoat," Hannah's
George is made "happy and tormented [as he] looked at the last of [Felice's]
foot going in the closing door many times over, gathered to the rail like a
great sinner at the bar" (*BOH,* 208). Felice *is* a maiden in distress, but her
bizarre and troubling situation is far from what George has imagined. He
can no more "read the signs" than can Joyce's character. George is soon "too
heavy in her story" (214); yet he continues to ignore the truth of his own
identity, as well as that of hers, as he imagines "high and valiant stuff"
(217) until he is stripped of his fantasy by the mundane truth of her love
affair with her elderly father-in-law.[21]

The incongruous merging of fiction and autobiography complicates the
narrative in *Boomerang,* where Hannah creates a version of himself and his
real-life wife and children and casts them opposite the fictional family of
Pat Yelverston, whose marriage has failed and whose son has been killed.
Yelverston is a financial success, but he describes himself by peripherals, as
"only . . . a man with big legs who had never stopped running from one
task toward another" (62). Thus, he is another in the long line of American
picaresques, of whom John Updike's "Rabbit" Angstrom is perhaps the
best-known contemporary model. Like the protagonist of *Ray,* who also
describes himself by peripheral details, both Rabbit and Yelverston are presented synechdochically by only their recurrent description as "running,"
suggesting a distorted, incomplete humanity that is "monstrous." In the
chapter of *Boomerang* entitled "Modern," the modern success stories of all
the characters are juxtaposed with stories of their conspicuous failures.
"Modern" concludes when the actual and fictional characters meet at the
celebration of Hannah's daughter Lee's college graduation. Apparently, in
the mind of the loosely autobiographical protagonist, Lee's name has con-
jured that of General Robert E. Lee and thus the Civil War, a subject never
far from the surface of any Hannah story. The final, seemingly illogical,

21. James Joyce, "Araby," *Dubliners* (1914; rpr. New York, 1984), 32.

sentence is this: "We're all so fucking terrible, no wonder it took four years of hideous war to get Lee up there and give up his sword" (64). Thus, what should have been closure on a successful episode of family life in fact opens up the ancient Confederate wound that ruptures when least expected for many southerners, even during brief victories.

Several characteristics of surfiction are apparent in "Upstairs, Mona Bayed for Dong," which begins self-reflexively (and what might seem illogically) *in medias res* with the sentence "Or give it another try, like a hot Hollywood novelist" (*BOH,* 265). Yet the passage that follows reveals the logic of the alleged rewrite, as it discloses the narrator's inability to tell a true story despite his repeated efforts to do so, undermining traditional notions of coherence or unity in the narration and the narrating self while also debunking any imagined poetic distance from the story. Novels by southern or other American writers have not always followed the "well-made" structure of the linear British norm, as Thomas Leitch points out, parenthetically noting the British novel's own "digressiveness, self-reflexiveness, and episodic resistance to closure" as far back as *Tristram Shandy.* The lyric short novels of such contemporary writers as Hannah bear witness to the influence of this tradition, represented in modern and contemporary literary history by the short story's obscure, nonlinear, and unresolved antithetical structure, as well as by its orality and general intertextuality—all marks of its debunking rhythm, and all consonant with the developing subgenre of postcontemporary surfiction and with postmodern poetics in general.[22]

Hannah is not a true surfictionist, although his development as a writer was during the 1960s and 1970s, the height of postmodernism. His links with the surfictionists are those of technique rather than perspective. He is more optimistic than the great Modernists, less cynical than most postcontemporary writers. He is by temperament a romantic writer—nostalgic and possessed of a great sadness, yet with what is perhaps an irrational optimism. Michael Malone, one of Hannah's most perceptive readers, observed twenty years ago that Hannah is "more romantic and less forgiving than Welty, though he does have the latter's sweetness of heart, her delight in the vitality of survivors," but that, like Faulkner, Hannah is also "moved by

---

22. Leitch, "The Debunking Rhythm of the American Short Story," in *Short Story Theory at a Crossroads,* ed. Lohafer and Clarey, 146.

macho romanticism." He writes with the great joy of a child in an unlimited toy store, except that his are linguistic "toys" found in the great storehouse of literary genres, techniques, and language. He is also a humorist, but his humor is that of the postmodern's irreverence rather than of the satirist's social gravity. Since I have likened Hannah's postmodern humor to that of writers as far distant in time as Laurence Sterne, I would agree with Lance Olsen that "postmodern humor has always been around to one degree or another . . . [and that it is] less a chronological fact than a . . . radically skeptical . . . state of mind that surfaces at various times and in various places—wacky graffiti on the walls of Rome, dark jokes in English monasteries . . . —whose impulse is to decenter, detotalize, and deconstruct while taking nothing—including its own (non)premises—very seriously." Hannah's greatest seriousness is in the writing, in the language; his great subject is the human comedy, emphasizing the frail but irrepressible human psyche and the comic spirit required to live in the postmodern world.[23]

23. Malone, "Everything That Rises," 706; Olsen, *Circus of the Mind in Motion,* 16, 27.

Four

Hannah's Comic Vision: Riffs on Language, Literature, and the "Play" of Life

The kind of tone I want is sometimes just a kind of confluence of music.
—Barry Hannah, interviewed by R. Vanarsdall

[Don Quixote] and Cervantes together evolve toward a new kind of literary dialectic. . . . What unites the Don and his squire is . . . their mutual participation in what has been called 'the order of play.' . . . Play is a voluntary activity, unlike madness and foolishness.
—Harold Bloom, *The Western Canon*

STORYTELLING IS A basic human need, according to both writers and literary theorists; and it is surely not beside the point that the telling of stories seems to have a connection to religious narrative—to the stories people have told since prehistoric times to try to explain the meaning of their own and the world's existence. Charles May, in discussing the origins of the short story, argues that "it is a form which has remained close to the primal narrative that embodies and recapitulates mythic perception . . . [and] is derived from folktale and myth." He points to Isak Dinesen's story "The Cardinal's First Tale," whose protagonist declares that "the divine art is the story. In the beginning was the story." Reynolds Price also sees the Bible as the primary source for narrative, and he calls narrative itself "the second most important need after food."[1]

It is not surprising that the need for story was strong for the first settlers in the American colonies; or that an important aspect of what became our literary history was the special need for humor; or that, given the "melting pot" nature of the new nation, its new stories represented the confluence of many "musics." In Constance Rourke's classic treatise on American humor, she asserts that comedy is "a lawless element, full of surprises . . . a matter of fantasy . . . [and that it] bears the closest relation to emotion, either bubbling up as from a deep and happy wellspring, or in an opposite fashion rising like a rebirth of feeling from dead levels after turmoil. An emotional man," she says, "may possess no humor, but a humorous man usually has deep pockets of emotion, sometimes tucked away or forgotten." This habit of forgetfulness was part of the earliest formative experiences of the American character, resulting, Rourke argues, from two separate needs: the need to mask uncomfortable experiences, for "in a primitive world crowded with pitfalls the unchanging, unaverted countenance had been a safeguard, preventing revelations of surprise, anger, or dismay"; and the need to evince the Puritan's solemn piety that led Governor William Bradford to direct Massachusetts Bay colonists to do their laughing in secret. But the developing nation, freed from theocracy, afforded new avenues for the comic aspect of American expression, not only as a social corrective for self-improvement but also for aesthetic reasons; as Henri Bergson notes, "The comic comes into being just when society and the individual, freed from the worry of self-preservation, begin to regard themselves as works of art."[2]

Just as Rourke traces the early American's bravado to the tumult of the Revolution, she traces a later facet of American humor to the War of 1812 and to the backwoodsmen whose tall tales depict them as "roarers": larger-than-life frontier heroes and fighters, Kentucky hunters come to do battle in New Orleans, who bragged in song that none wished their "little force

1. Charles E. May, "Metaphoric Motivation in Short Fiction: 'In the Beginning Was the Story,'" in *Short Story Theory at a Crossroads,* ed. Lohafer and Clarey, 62; Reynolds Price, quoted in Susan Ketchin, *The Christ-Haunted Landscape: Faith and Doubt in Southern Fiction* (Jackson, Miss., 1994), 57.

2. Constance Rourke, *American Humor* (New York, 1931), ix, 9–11; Henri Bergson, "Laughter," in *Comedy,* ed. Wylie Sypher (1956; Baltimore, 1980), 73.

. . . to be greater, / For every man was half a horse and half an alligator." The flatboatmen on the Mississippi added to the eighteenth- and early-nineteenth-century lore by their tales of heroic exploits as they overcame the "horror, terror, and death [which] were writ large in the life of rivers and forests," tales that were told in "a comic oblivious tone." Of course, the tall tale's hyperbolic character lends itself to great freedom in the use of language, including oratory, but it also includes "sudden comic shouts or mock pompous words" and tellers who "lie from the delight of invention and the charm of fictitious narrative." For these backwoodsmen, Rourke says, "the truth was too small."[3]

The complex nature of Barry Hannah's humor has deep roots in these American literary traditions, to which he brings his unique comic vision. The situational humor in his fiction, which runs the gamut from slapstick burlesque to parody and the absurd and from the malappropriate to the Gothic grotesque and macabre, provides a fertile field for linguistic and other kinds of textual, often intertextual, play. His fiction's ancestry lies not only in southern and southwest humor, traditions with an equal basis in social satire and democratic individualism, but also in the techniques of linguistic improvisation that link the most venerable comic novel in the Western canon, Cervantes' *Don Quixote*, to texts of the postmodern movement. Thus, his literary vision bears witness to the distinction between the more critical nature of satirical humor and the more disinterested, playful nature of the comic, through which *homo ludens*, "man playing," celebrates life and defies death. *More* is a key term here, because the distinction, both in Hannah and in literary history in general, is not absolute but one of degree.

Hannah's humor makes an oblique commentary on society, but his fiction resonates not with cultural correctives but with the exuberance of the poet's poet. His humor is certainly "lawless" in its disregard of political correctness in language and content; but of course, the nature of humor in general is its lawless, subversive attack on anyone or anything that the humorist believes is taken too seriously or exerts undue pressure. The most aggressive humor is often sexist, racist, or homophobic—reflecting deeply personal, perhaps visceral, responses to culture—or it may parody those who are sexist, racist, homophobic, or perhaps merely annoying. In this

---

3. Rourke, *American Humor,* 35–39, 61–68.

way, humor also masks aggression, as Freud showed in his *Jokes and Their Relation to the Unconscious*. Thus, a major vein in American humor is associated with various "others"; in Hannah's fiction, as Allen Shepherd notes, "Outlanders are sometimes viewed with distaste and suspicion." As evidence, Shepherd cites "The Time," a chapter in *Boomerang* in which the narrator complains about "those Arabs [who] own the oil and . . . come over here wanting the other end of the pump . . . [and] white dumb wives, some of them'" (79). He also recites, from *Boomerang*, the narrator's "enemies list," which includes "frowning fat Christians" (18); and he observes that "readers just shouldn't expect Hannah to . . . endow women with a metaphysical significance even distantly approaching his own." Like most humorists, Hannah thickens the texture of his writing with in-jokes based on personal life, culture, and history, and with in-texts—intertextual references to other works of literature. Everywhere apparent in his fiction is the influence of the humorists of the southwest frontier, a tradition that actually began with southerners like Augustus Baldwin Longstreet and George Washington Harris and that is exemplified by Twain, who, as Lewis Simpson reminds us, "made the comic interpretation of life in the South germane to the whole literary vision of the American negotiation between dream and history."[4]

Under Hannah's pen, even the Gothic grotesque serves the comic vision; one of his funniest uses of this mode is his parody, in *The Tennis Handsome*, of Faulkner's *As I Lay Dying*. In the chapter entitled "The Redemptress Exhibition," Bobby Smith has decided to follow his tennis idol, French Edward, to see him play in New Orleans at the Redemptress High School gym. Having recently been rejected by his aunt and sometime lover, Bobby seeks out the company of Dr. James Word, who has loved and lost French Edward's mother. On the way, Word apparently has heart palpitations, and during the match he tries to cheer for French but "sat back down, holding his heart" (131). In the parking lot soon after the match, Dr. Word dies. Bobby simply props the corpse up in the car and starts toward Vicksburg and home; but along the way he turns toward the Mississippi River and

---

4. Freud, quoted in Don Anderson, "Comic Modes in Modern American Fiction," *Southern Review* (University of Adelaide, Australia), VII (1974), 155; Shepherd, "'Something Wonderful to Tell,'" 75–76, 78; Lewis P. Simpson, Introduction to Part I of *The History of Southern Literature*, ed. Louis D. Rubin, Jr., *et al.* (Baton Rouge, 1985), 12.

throws the body off a bridge. The next chapter, "The Old Flit Floats to New Orleans," begins with a parody of Faulkner's already grotesquely humorous scene, in *As I Lay Dying,* of the flood that overturns Addie Bundren's coffin and floats it down the river. Hannah's narrative is presented through the imagination of Baby Levaster, whose "daylight nightmares had become too vivid" (133):

> Dr. Word was so dried out and light-boned, he floated on his back down toward New Orleans, bobbing in the drift, turning slowly around. But some leftover mad alligator below Natchez got to him. When he floated by Baton Rouge, he looked like a harmonica—his ribs, etc. Some casual darkie, alone on the levee, playing his tonette, may have seen a weird roil in the Big Muddy, a rolling of bones and cloth shreds.
>
> Word slept with the fish. Like them, he made friends with the continental sewage of the Mississippi. Clouds rammed together in a flatulence of atmospherics. Lightning knocked the hell out of nothing. Then the rain came so hard, it stood up his corpse and the corpse began walking, sometimes almost water-skiing when a gust hit it just right. Then the corpse, impatient, strode on the water.
>
> Word was making fast time. In a week, he would be at the Three Fingers Saloon, where Levaster was thinking all this and staring at the silent French Edward. (133)

The short sentence "Dr. Word slept with the fish" suggests Vardaman's "My mother is a fish"; and the description of Word's body as "cloth shreds" suggests Tull's description of Cash, struggling in the river, who "looked just like a old bundle of clothes kind of washing up and down against the bank." The most telling image is, of course, Word's upright corpse, which seems to be walking on the storm-tossed river, and thus which parodies the log in *As I Lay Dying,* which "stood for an instant upright upon that surging and heaving desolation like Christ," eventually "strik[ing the wagon], tilting it up and on," and plunging Addie's coffin into the water. Hannah's contemporary version of this comedy allows for the water-skiing metaphor. He follows the modernist technique Faulkner employed in *The Sound and the Fury* and *As I Lay Dying,* presenting the story through the subjective perspectives of multiple characters. Hannah also follows his own postmodern bent with a narrative that, after building a scene, calls into question its ever happening at all, as he does here through Baby Levaster's "too vivid" imagination and through the use of the present progressive tense, which describes the corpse's "making fast time" at the same moment that Baby is "thinking all this." Such a blend of narrative techniques helps to demonstrate Faulkner's modernist influence on Hannah while it also links Hannah with postmodernist techniques such as, for example, those of Tim O'Brien in *Going after Cacciato.*[5]

Hannah's comic vision, which is revealed in a narrative form that is somewhere between dream/nightmare and history/story, is routinely mentioned in critical assessments of his fiction, but we do not yet adequately understand it. David Madden, commenting on Hannah's having developed a short story into a chapter of *Geronimo Rex,* said that "the early sophomoric cuteness of 'The Crowd Punk Season Drew' [had] been transmuted into a mature wittiness" in his first novel. In his reading of "Love Too Long," Allen Shepherd describes a comic pattern that "preserves our pleasure in the narrator's distress by a combination of sheer manic inventiveness and formulaic sequences in which bad plus worse somehow always equals worst." Shepherd expresses disappointment, however, in *Captain Maximus,* arguing that Hannah had "turned exceedingly cryptic, abrupt and jokey," so that the lack of plot and characterization and his stories' strange settings leave the reader "dependent on voice, style, manic language" . . . [and are only] occasionally entertaining." Donald Noble writes that *Airships* is made up of "largely funny stories, but [that] it is often gallows humor, as if there is literally nothing else to do but laugh; conditions are too bleak for anything else."[6]

The play of language is the one thing remarked by all commentators on Hannah's fiction, and it is something Hannah has developed intentionally, beginning with the shift from third-person omniscient point of view in "The Crowd Punk Season Drew" to the more intimate and idiosyncratic first-person point of view in *Geronimo Rex.* In a lesson for developing writers, Madden quotes both versions of the same scene to demonstrate the

5. William Faulkner, *As I Lay Dying* (1930; rpr. New York, 1990), 84, 155, 148.
6. Madden, "Barry Hannah's *Geronimo Rex* in Retrospect," 309; Shepherd, "Outrage and Speculation," 67; Allen Shepherd, "The Latest Whiz-Bang: Barry Hannah's *Captain Maximus,*" *Notes on Mississippi Writers,* XIX (1987), 29, 31; Noble, " 'Tragic and Meaningful to An Insane Degree,' " 43.

difference in style; he shows, for example, that third-person omniscient "produces a rather formal, stilted style, despite the author's own slangy direct comments about his protagonist . . . [while] it is enhanced in the revision by dramatic immediacy, and a kind of frenzy, and a certain obnoxious aggressiveness that catches and holds the reader's attention." Thus, in the original story, the passage "Buicks, Pontiacs, and Fords with eccentric horsepower and conveniences—he scarred them all," becomes, in the novel:

> I was standing beside a skyblue Cadillac. You pretentious whale, you Cadillac, I thought.
> I jumped up on the hood of it. I did a shuffle on the hood. I felt my boots sinking into the metal. "Ah!" (*GR*, 232)[7]

In this passage, as in Hannah's work as a whole, the development is from more straightforward descriptions by means of adjectives, in this case the adjectival phrase "with eccentric horsepower and conveniences," which modifies the list of automobiles, to metaphor: "You pretentious whale, you Cadillac." In addition to Hannah's substitution of direct, factual description with a comparison that juxtaposes two terms without a logical transition, a stylistic disjunction appropriate to poetry as well as to a postmodern poetics, there is the incongruity of his having the narrator speak directly to either a Cadillac or a whale. The humor is due in part to the ironic distance gained by the changed dynamic: instead of a direct address by storyteller to rational audience (reader), the text provides a direct address by narrator to irrational audience (Cadillac/whale), while the reader/voyeur observes Harry's sophomoric frenzy.

By the time he wrote *Airships, Ray,* and *Boomerang,* Hannah had fully developed the short-circuit technique common to disjunctive discourse, to the point that he could write a history of the world in one paragraph:

> Before us there were tribes of people wandering around deciding what to eat or fuck or own. Billions of people went across this planet, asking each other "Did you get any last night?" Then came religion and all the long-winded phony bastards like Plato. The guy that wrote Leviticus should be shot for

---

7. David Madden, *Revising Fiction: A Handbook for Writers* (New York, 1988), 26; Madden quotes Hannah's "The Crowd Punk Season Drew," from *Intro,* I (1968).

boredom. Then came gunpowder and steel. The Europeans occurred with tea and gunpowder. Some of the afternoons were tedious and so they began killing thousands of each other to own shit. Then came Pearl Harbor. Then came America and Uncle Joe, who only killed seven million of his own people for, get this, an idea. Commie against Free. The preachers are still going at it. Jimmy Swaggart said on the television that he would sweep out a lonely mission with a broom for the rest of his life if that's what God called him to do. He liked to "make love" to a New Orleans prostitute while her little daughter watched. I dare the man to quit Baton Rouge and sweep out a lonely mission for the rest of his life. I dare him. If he will do that I'll fly down to where he is and play him some of those hellish tapes of his cousin Jerry Lee Lewis and help him sweep. (*B*, 67–68)

In keeping with comedy's tendency toward in-jokes, this passage is most humorous to those who know something of the history it purports to relate. From "Pearl Harbor" this history jump-cuts to "America and Uncle Joe [Stalin], who only killed seven million of his own people," thus representing the entirety of World War II by two of its darkest moments: the sneak attack by Japan on the U.S. fleet in Hawaii and the betrayal of the Allies in Europe by Joseph Stalin. Significantly, "America" is sandwiched between these two subversive incidents, Hannah rendering with poetic accuracy the general time frame of this country's participation in the war. Beyond the ironic understatement of "only," which ungrammatically is meant to modify "seven million ... people," another mode of irony at work in the passage is the comic technique of romantic irony, a means of achieving aesthetic distance, described by Coleridge as that which makes "our great appear little and our little great; or rather, which reduces to a common littleness both the great and the little, when compared to infinity." Hannah's romantic irony is directed at the "great" World War II and its "great" leaders: Stalin's betrayal of "his own people ... for ... an idea" is deflated by what amounts to a dramatic "aside" in "get this." "Religion" is telescoped from "long-winded phony bastards like Plato" to the contemporary televangelism scandals of one preacher, to which fully one third of Hannah's "history" is devoted. A version of romantic irony is also constituted by the reduction of "Europeans" to their metonymic representation by "tea and gunpowder," and by the more general metonym of all people as characterized by what they "eat or fuck or own." Moreover, that the record of an entire culture is accomplished by the one verb "occurred" contributes to a short-circuit description that is humorously enhanced by the added illogic of Eliotic "tedious . . . afternoons" as the reason for these Europeans' "kill[ing] thousands of each other to own shit." Hannah presents his "history" in terms of the most reprehensible actions and the lowest forms of human motivation for action: decisions about "what to eat or fuck or own." There is nothing so serious or so "great" that it is not fair game for deflation by Hannah's biting, in this case sardonic, wit.[8]

The place of obscenity in Hannah's language-based humor, while partly explained by Coleridge's concept of romantic irony, is made more relevant to the world of Hannah's characters by Norman Mailer's similar theory of American humor. Mailer explains it in his "non-fiction novel" *Armies of the Night,* his third-person account of his participation in the October 21, 1967, march on the Pentagon to protest the Vietnam War:

> There was no villainy in obscenity for him, just—paradoxically, characteristically—his love for America: he had first come to love America when he served in the U.S. Army, not the America of course of the flag, the patriotic unendurable fix of the television programs and the newspapers, no, long before he was ever aware of the institutional oleo of the most suffocating American ideas he had come to love what editorial writers were fond of calling the democratic principle with its faith in the common man. He found that principle and that man in the Army, but what none of the editorial writers ever mentioned was that the noble common man was obscene as an old goat, and his obscenity was what saved him. The sanity of said common democratic man was in his humor, his humor was in his obscenity.[9]

Many of Hannah's most important fictional characters, not only those in the military, represent the "noble common man." If they are as "obscene as . . . old goat[s]," it is at least in part their humorous obscenity that saves them. Such humor is everywhere in Hannah's fiction: in the language of adolescents trying out the language; in story titles like "Upstairs, Mona Bayed for Dong"; in sustained passages and entire stories like "Dragged

8. Samuel Taylor Coleridge, *Miscellaneous Criticism,* ed. Thomas Middleton Raysor (1931; rpr. Cambridge, Mass., 1936), 113.

9. Norman Mailer, *Armies of the Night: History as a Novel, the Novel as History* (1968; rpr. New York, 1994), 47.

Fighting from His Tomb"; and in throwaway comments like that of Harry Monroe in "Mother Rooney Unscrolls the Hurt," when asked if "the Irish have a music." Monroe, in this story a student at Millsaps College who "took a lot of courses in music," answers that the Irish "have a uniform national fart" (*A,* 190).

Some of Hannah's language-based humor results from the juxtaposition of two levels of diction or from a level of diction that is inappropriate to the situation it describes. In "Snerd and Niggero," for example, the illicit passions of the unromantically named "Mrs. Niggero . . . [and] Mr. Snerd on the couch" are described by language that is a dispassionate mixture, strangely formal, yet with the effect of jargon. As their lovemaking progresses, "her dress was as a rolled flag around her neck and one cup of her brassiere was hanging off her left globe . . . [when] Snerd . . . with resignation pushed in amidperson, a little deaf with grief and wild comfort . . . and the two of them settled into the planes of full criminal love, pulling each the other's organ from its aim and both losing; something like a pilgrim running back and forth through the doorway of a shrine, welcomed then ejected" (*HL,* 81–82). Moreover, what could have been a poignant, if unlikely, story of a husband and a lover grieving together weeks after Nancy Niggero's death is undercut by Hannah's presentation of the whole affair as a burlesque. The husband, a Bartleby-like man at his desk with "an old-fashioned clerk's eyeshade he imagined touched him with romance in accuracy . . . for twenty-seven years had been driven pale and near emaciated" by his job, by his "lupine rapture" for his wife, and by his unspoken desire to shout to her: "Please stomp on my grapes!" (83–85). At the end of the story the narrative assumes a plaintive tone, noting that "in the next fifteen years, before Snerd died . . . the two men enjoyed a friendship"; but this, too, is deflated by the interjection of malappropriate word juxtaposition and by ironic understatement presented as hyperbole: Snerd was "buried promptly by his wife, who remarried avidly," and the men's remarkable friendship was "such as had hardly been known in the whole north part of the state, and even up through Memphis" (89).

Sometimes, as in the "history of the world" paragraph, the linguistic humor is pervasive in Hannah's fiction; at other times, it surfaces briefly in the midst of what otherwise seems noncomic material. In Hannah, however, one is never far from comedy. In "Two Gone Over," the tone of the narrator's passion for the "girl from Tallahassee" (*HL,* 170) shifts rapidly from poignant realism, in his admission that "her forehead was touched around by brown bangs that made [his] stomach ache" (169); to a linguistic zinger about "her belly-dropping legs" (171); and then again to an even greater poignancy, depicted in a lyrical dream-vision of "all the frigid black wind of the Dakota night, all that black wind between the places you have left behind that don't want you anymore" (171).

Since the stability of ironic humor depends on shared cultural knowledge, some readers may need help in decoding Hannah's work, which is deeply rooted in his own generation, region, and such personal interests as music, military history, and, of course, the craft of writing. In terms of music, for example, his many musician and other artist characters and his explicit use of musical terms in describing his fiction provide a constant frame of reference. "Music," Hannah told Scott Cawelti, "remains the ultimate act to me, I love it because there's no comment after good music." In particular, Hannah is affected by the popular music of his "quasi-hippie" days, and what he calls the "moral" music of that era still speaks to him more than does any music of the present day: "I grew up with Jimi [Hendrix] and Janis [Joplin] and Miles Davis, Bob Dylan, true poets, screamers and musicians. And now I see Guns n' Roses. Any garage band in my town could have whipped them, given the amount of equipment. Very rarely do Guns 'n Roses come out with anything worth getting excited about, even for a good revolt. Whereas I thought the first ones did, The Who, and Jimi Hendrix. Also they just played the hell out of it. A few of the young guys really get to me—Van Halen, a laudable technician. But I think it's a wasteland. I feel like *Father Knows Best.*" That Hannah still identifies with the "screamers" he idolized in his youth is suggested in one way by his emblematic use of the "Screaming Rebel Rocket" on the dust jackets of *Bats Out of Hell* and *High Lonesome.* That some of his most appreciative readers also see the connection is clear; for example, in a review of *Bats Out of Hell,* Will Blythe compares Hannah with Jimi Hendrix, asserting that "what Hendrix did with the guitar, Hannah does with prose: invent a whole new American music, viciously electric, of squawks and cries, of soul rhythms and extraterrestrial riffs."[10]

Hannah's own use of the term *riff* indicates the ease with which he trans-

10. Cawelti, "An Interview With Barry Hannah," 107–108; Will Blythe, "Hannah and His Sentences," *Esquire* (March, 1993), 55.

poses musical to literary terms, as it also reflects the important subtext in his fiction that music and musicians constitute. When interviewed by Tom Vitale, Hannah said that in writing his Ozark folktale, "Evening of the Yarp: A Report By Roonswent Dover," he was "doing a riff on mountain boys and that civilization" in the Arkansas hill country. Much modernist and postmodernist literature, of course, is replete with such in-texts, and especially those with anchors in either music or the painterly arts. One thinks immediately of the important musical bases of James Baldwin's "Sonny's Blues" and, among southern writers, of Eudora Welty's "Power-house" and Fred Chappell's "Blue Dive." When John Griffin Jones asked Hannah about the influence of other southern writers, his answer began with a reference to music: "If you read something like 'Powerhouse' by Miss Welty and you were a young musician something's got to rub off. That's a powerful piece of jazz work. It's amazing—and I hope that women won't feel bad about this . . . —and this is not an antiwoman statement, but I am shocked that a woman knew that much about a traveling musician. Just shocked!"[11]

Donald R. Noble, who also experiences Hannah's fiction in terms of music, has contributed one of the few published insights to date on the mechanics of the author's narrative techniques. While noting that Hannah's characters in *Geronimo Rex, Nightwatchmen,* and *Airships* comment on the outrages of their lives, Noble observes that

> it is the language of their running commentary on their existence that is Hannah's greatest gift, beyond characterization or his sometimes thin plots; it is always *the voice* that holds the reader, and the way that voice uses language. Hannah's narrative voice is a jazz speaker. The voice *knows* language, syntax, the exact meaning of words in the way that a musician knows how to play every note precisely and for the proper length of time. . . . Hannah's voice *bends* language; the meanings of words are stretched so that one has never seen the words used in quite that way before. Ray says of his nurse, "I began lying to her lavishly." (*R,* 111)

Noble also points out that Hannah's characters "find release and accomplishment in music, especially in jazz and raucous rock." In an interview

---

11. Vitale, interview with Barry Hannah; Hannah, quoted in Jones, "Barry Hannah," 141.

with R. Vanarsdall for the *Southern Review,* Hannah again describes his
writing in terms of music: "The kind of tone I want is sometimes just a
kind of confluence of music. I keep my music box here, put on some [Jimi]
Hendrix or something, you know how music will evoke a whole [period of
time, perhaps several] . . . months of some year that has passed . . . [and]
will bring back things very visually." Thus, for Hannah, as for blues and
jazz artist characters like Welty's Powerhouse, music is a narrative act; con-
versely, for great instrumentalists of language, such as Baldwin, Welty,
Chappell, and Hannah, narrative plays like music.[12]

Neither jazz, blues, nor "raucous rock" is appreciated by everyone—and
neither, Hannah knows, are his stories. Like other postmodernist fiction,
his is in some ways elitist; thus he does not scruple to use in-jokes that most
readers are not meant to "get," including those resulting from his creation
of characters who are thinly veiled, oblique versions of people in the Clinton, Mississippi, of his youth. In "Testimony of Pilot," for example, he
makes a dead hero of the band-director character Dick Prender, one of several instances in which Hannah creates a cameo for Dick Prenshaw, his
own high-school band director. Reading the story of the fictional teacher's
untimely demise in a wreck one foggy night on the way to a band concert,
one can imagine Hannah and the real-life character models laughing together at the campy melodrama of the scene in which the band plays on in
director Prender's memory. In the story, Ard Quadberry plays his horn
while he leads the band, "a weeping herd" (*A*, 27), although he is also "very
much afflicted, almost to the point of drooling by a love and respect for
Dick Prender, and now afflicted by a heartbreaking esteem for his ghost"
(26).[13]

Clearly, Hannah is having more fun than anyone with his writing, although his enjoyment must be as double-edged as are some of the tragi-
comic episodes he relates. From *Geronimo Rex* on, it has been clear that his
protagonists mask their uncertainties and deep emotions with humorous

12. Noble, "'Tragic and Meaningful to an Insane Degree,'" 38, 40, Noble's emphasis;
Hannah, quoted in Vanarsdall, "The Spirits Will Win Through," 326, Hannah's ellipses.

13. In "Fire over the Town," a humorous one-page narrative somewhere between fiction
and fact, in *Southern Living* (October, 1982), 138, Hannah writes, "Then the great Prenshaw
came to direct the band, and my high school years had a hero, an actual living adult that one
would follow into flames."

pranks, outrageous language, blatant and noisy lies and, in Rourke's words, "a comic oblivious tone." At the same time, they see themselves as "works of art," in that they are vain and they are constantly creating and re-creating themselves. In a fiction that is loosely autobiographical, then, Hannah has essentially reimagined himself—or parts of himself—in many of the characters, playing role after role as he writes, while tilting against his private windmills. Certainly his fictional world, like that in the early humor writing Rourke describes, is filled with horror, violence, verbal hyperbole, and fantastic situations. Hannah's stories, however, the western and war fiction in particular, read more like Chaplinesque rewrites of the surrealities of Stephen Crane or Ambrose Bierce. Their elitism is only minimally the result of cryptic autobiographical allusions; more precisely, it is a literary elitism that depends on one's knowledge of literature and language and on one's willingness to play the game.

In an Australian journal article on comic modes in American fiction, Don Anderson argues that although the Western canon has long promoted the tragic modes as the sine qua non of literary achievement, major modernist authors such as Faulkner and Joyce show that "there is nothing necessary about tragedy" and, moreover, that for contemporary authors like Nabokov and Barth, "a purely heroic or tragic or romantic vision of affairs is no longer possible." Anderson points up the passage in Faulkner's *Light in August* in which Byron Bunch describes the corpse of Joanna Burden, the head of which "was turned clean around like she was looking behind her." Bunch logically believes that if Miss Burden "could just have done that when she was alive, she might not have been doing it now." The comic response modifies what otherwise might have been a scene of unrelieved Gothic horror. This scene is foreshadowed by a previous one in the subplot that Anderson calls "a comic version of the same sentiment," when Lena Grove, heavily pregnant with Lucas Burch's child, begins her search for him by going through the same window that she had climbed out nightly to meet him, and thinks, "If it had been this hard to do before, I reckon I would not be doing it now." Moreover, although Anderson does not cite it, the last-mentioned scene has been prepared for by an even earlier narrative comment that "she had lived there eight years before she opened the window for the first time . . . [and] she had not opened it a dozen times hardly before she discovered that she should not have opened it at all." In other words, pity and terror are not the only possible responses to Faulkner, and even the gruesome depiction of the unfortunate Miss Burden's head "cannot be dismissed as sick, Gothic, or merely in bad taste." Such works imply that existence is "no longer registered as tragic, or purely tragic." They depict a response to life that is not despair but rather a system of play "by *creating* in the face of chaos; that is," Anderson says, "by constructing elaborate games."[14]

Hannah contributes to this tradition of creative game playing in important ways. He continues in the lineage of southern humor by parodying the southern Gothic, the heroic epic, and the western romance and by parodying the styles of many individual writers he admires. In part through his extensive use of parody, he participates in the ancient traditions represented by carnival. As Mikhail M. Bakhtin explains in tracing the use of carnivalesque traditions in Rabelais, the stock characters of "popular-festive forms" of communal activity like Mardi Gras include such "gay monsters" as the king who is dethroned and then abused as a clown. This metamorphosis symbolizes the death of the old year or season and the birth of the new. "Abuse with uncrowning, as truth about the old authority, about the dying world, is an organic part of Rabelais' system of images," Bakhtin argues, a system that also includes the carnivalesque characteristics of "the Gospel story of the mock crowning, uncrowning, and scourging of 'the king of the Jews.' " Other characters in these festivals are contrasting comic pairs, such as Don Quixote and Sancho Panza. Hannah's comic vision includes not only devices such as "gay monsters" and comic pairs but also the customary grotesque violence to the carnival victim and the sexual content that bespeaks carnival's emphasis on fertility and rebirth. According to Bakhtin, "There is no pure abstract negation in the popular-festive system of images; it tends to embrace both poles of becoming in their contradiction and unity. The one who is thrashed or slaughtered is decorated. The beating itself has a gay character; it is introduced and concluded with laughter. . . . [Such beatings are] . . . no ordinary fight[s], no commonplace blows administered in everyday life. The blows have . . . a broadened, sym-

14. William Faulkner, *Light in August* (1932; rpr. New York, 1968), 85, 4, 3; Anderson, "Comic Modes in Modern American Fiction," 152–53, 155, emphasis Anderson's.

bolic, ambivalent meaning; they at once kill and regenerate, put an end to the old life and start the new. . . . [Such an] episode is filled with a bacchic atmosphere."[15]

Aspects of the carnivalesque are found in many of Hannah's stories, often in the form of a much-abused victim whose agony resembles that of Christ. It is reflected, for example, even in the title of "The Agony of T. Bandini," the story of Tiger Bandini, who "felt shunned" (*HL,* 128) and is publicly beaten, and who has "a free, wide heart for the vanquished" (130). It is even more significant in "Drummer Down," in which the carpenter "Drum at his death was sixty-six, twice the age of Christ at Golgotha" (*HL,* 196). Drum, we are told, "spoke often of 'love' and 'quest' . . . [and] prefaced many things he said with 'I am a Christian,' sadly, as if he were in some dreadful losers' club" (197). "Drummer Down" is a third-person narrative but is told through the central consciousness of Paul Smith, sometime professor of creative writing and Drum's teacher. It is clear, however, that Smith is equally a disciple of Drum, and thus they are alter egos. When Smith's drunkenness and general neglect of his job get him fired and also "barred from his old home" (202), his lifestyle becomes even more degenerate. He lives with a series of parasitic students and bad musicians, and he wears nothing but an "SS overcoat . . . with a Maltese cross made by Drum hanging from a chain around his neck, [and] he had grown so thin that his wedding band had fallen off somewhere. He was now almost pure spirit" (202–203). The important carnivalistic device here is Drum as a martyr who is repeatedly abused but whose very presence seems to regenerate and heighten the existence of those around him. Smith sees him as "a kitchen God" (200). Drum is also like Jesus in that he leaves no written evidence of the faith he inspired; thus Smith is "angry a long time that Drum had left nothing else . . . [but a poem that was only] a common piece of trash off a bathroom wall" (209).

Hannah's most recent novel, *Never Die,* constitutes his most extensive use of the carnivalesque and its theme of regeneration through violence. In this hilarious but dark parody of the western novel and its myth of the law-

15. Mikhail M. Bakhtin, *Rabelais and His World,* trans. Helene Iswolsky (Bloomington, Ind., 1984), 197–203, 205.

less Old West, Hannah conducts a veritable clinic on postmodern humor, at the same time continuing in the Huck Finn tradition of that peculiarly American adaptation of the male quest narrative, in which, to repeat Leslie Fiedler's phrase, "good bad boys" like Huck Finn "light out for the Territory," heading west from civilization. Mary Gordon notes the centrality of this running boy figure in American literature as she discusses *Light in August,* citing Faulkner's description of the "fine shape of eternal youth and virginal desire which makes heroes." Gordon says that motion "is the boy's genius. He *must* be able to move. Move freely. Quickly. The boy on his strong legs cuts through the world, through time, constricting space, the accidents of birth, class, limitation, law. He wriggles out from under the crushing burden of fate. And fate's agent, the embodiment of unmoving weight, is female. She who does not move, who will not move, who cannot move. Who won't allow the boy to move." Throughout the literature of the nineteenth century, the prevailing direction of American running males had been west. Hannah is one of a growing number of contemporary southern novelists who have begun to write westerns, recalling either that first great era of westward pioneering or the early or mid-twentieth century, when some vestiges of the frontier remained, for example, on the Texas-Mexico border that is the setting of some Cormac McCarthy novels. *Never Die,* the story of a good bad boy gone west, has the uncanny sense of a more violent version of Crane's "The Bride Comes to Yellow Sky," which contrasts the manly West with the feminizing influence of civilization and depicts the relationship between sheriff and renegade as a game in which each enjoys his role until the bride comes to spoil it. But whereas "Yellow Sky," despite its impressionist techniques and its theme of game playing, exhibits the traditional bell-shaped plot, *Never Die* is more nearly the postmodernist novel as wordplay: closer in spirit to the works of Nabokov, Borges, Barth, and Barthelme.[16]

Hannah's novel pits would-be hero Fernando Muré against dastardly villain Kyle Nitburg and company. Nitburg has "continued to cheat, lie and steal [until] . . . pretty soon the town and much land around it was his,"

16. Faulkner, *Light in August,* 458; Mary Gordon, *Good Boys and Dead Girls* (New York, 1991), 3–4, emphasis Gordon's. Don Anderson, in "Comic Modes in Modern American Fiction," 157, describes the work of these postmoderns in terms of "the novel as game-world."

and he has been established as the mayor of what is now called Nitburg. Enter university-educated gunfighter Muré, he of the "dancing testicles named Juan and Manuel" (*ND*, 6). The fast-paced story follows Fernando's career as his macho swagger is demolished when both his knees are crushed by Nitburg's hit man, a dwarf named Smoot, and he plots to avenge himself. In the section entitled "1911," Nitburg echoes Crane's Scratchy Wilson when he laments, "There used to be gunplay here. There's hardly any now, you notice" (48). Hannah's villain quickly corrects himself, however, painting a darker and ultimately more realistic picture of the Old West, despite this novel's use of it in farce. "Actually," he admits, "there wasn't much . . . play. People shot each other, from the back at close range, preferably. One true pistolero came in the territory, you wouldn't hear a peep for weeks. You could say I was the first to introduce . . . an unpistoled dwarf as . . . regulator. You can't just have Law, Smoot. You've got to have something *of the night,* you understand?" (48; ellipsis Hannah's). Nitburg's expression "something of the night," which echoes a phrase from Djuna Barnes's *Nightwood,* a darkly comic modernist novel in which important subtexts are night and watchers, evinces the seemingly inexhaustible intertextuality that allows Hannah to draw on linguistic resources from many literary eras and styles for use in a single story.[17]

His parody of Crane's story continues when Scratchy, the town drunk of Yellow Sky, with his "maroon-colored flannel shirt" is echoed in *Never Die* in the hermit Nermer's red shirt and belief in guns. Nermer says to Fernando, "Ain't barely a point to the West if you can't have a beet-colored pistolero outfit like that, is there? With that silver hand-rifle" (54). Similarly, as Scratchy says to his "ancient antagonist," Jack Potter, "Don't you tell me you ain't got no gun on you, you whelp," so Nermer "looked for a short-gun somewhere on [Fernando]" (54). Hannah's hero *does* have a gun, but his quick-draw technique is more appropriate to the mechanical violence of a cartoon from Saturday morning television:

> The guitar flew from his right hand and Fernando did a backflip on the soil flat off the ground in front of Nermer. Next thing Nermer knew, his hat had flown backward and the barrel of a short-gun was in his mouth, Fernando

17. Djuna Barnes, *Nightwood* (1936; rpr. New York, 1961), 161.

smiling over him and himself thrown rearward and the man's other arm under his back, his own pistol cast away with his hand making a claw in the
empty air for it.

—Jesus, even I couldn't miss you like this, could I? grinned Fernando.
(54–55)

Toward the end of *Never Die*, a minor character even articulates the implicit theme of "The Bride Comes to Yellow Sky": "Maybe it's the last of
something, said the German. Your damned woolly West" (148).[18]

Another indication of Hannah's adaptation of Crane is that Fernando,
like Jack Potter, "was a gunfighter almost without intending to be" (3).
Furthermore, as an ostensibly peaceable man, he is also a parody of the classic western fictional lawman as peace officer, such as the stoic John Wayne
or *Gunsmoke*'s imperturbable Matt Dillon. And just as Marshall Dillon has
an implicit relationship with the saloon owner, Miss Kitty, Fernando has a
"constant girlfriend, Stella, a slut with tuberculosis" (6), whose ultimate
model is no doubt Dulcinea, the prostitute sweetheart of Don Quixote.
The Don, of course, with sidekick Sancho Panza, constitutes the comic
pair that is the model for that American heroic pair of radio and motion
pictures, the Lone Ranger and his "faithful companion," Tonto. That
Hannah has not overlooked this connection is clear from the several repeti-
tions in the novel of the question "Who *was* that man?" (57), echoing the
now-famous ending line from each weekly episode of the radio serial, as the
Lone Ranger and Tonto rode off into the sunset: "Who *was* that masked
man?" Hannah's pairs, however, compared to the Lone Ranger and Tonto,
are "something of the night"; for they include Nitburg and Smoot as well
as Muré and Nermer. Hannah's use of the archetypal pair in *Never Die* is in
the true comic spirit of carnival, which depicts the incongruous combination that provokes laughter, even as it shows the grotesque violence that accompanies change.

Since Fernando is the far-from-stoic center of consciousness in *Never
Die*, we are privy to a continuing recitation of his hopes and fears. His
thoughts and those of other characters are often the vehicles for Hannah's

18. Stephen Crane, "The Bride Comes to Yellow Sky," in *Heath Anthology of American
Literature*, ed. Paul Lauter *et al.* (2nd ed.; 2 vols.; Lexington, Mass., 1994), II, 736–38.

ironic humor. For example, during the grand final battle of heroes and villains, would-be heroes and other pretenders, Doc Fingo cowers in his office
at "the first report of gunfire" (136). When a bullet hits his window, his reaction shows a comic version of the cultural concern with honor and shame
that is seen in other Hannah stories, especially those set in the South. The
irony here is uncharacteristically gentle for Hannah, especially in this violent novel, as though it masks an authorial nostalgia for the Wild West or
for a child's pleasure in "playing cowboy":

> Fingo was taken by pleasant inner visions of manly gunfire outdoors. . . .
> War has its romance, too, he mused. Rather cozy here, as men burst back and
> forth at each other, snapping metal. He heard something like a salvo just feet
> away. He was there, in the manly world of men and armed conflict! He
> pushed a finger above the desk top as a wistful target, feeling he was full in
> the fray, actually leading a sort of opiated assault on the army of his own
> shame. He was in it, he was off into it! He had a sort of cavalry in his ears,
> his own craven blood pouting away. Fingo once mended a broken dog and
> dwelled with the heroism of that act." (137)

Fingo's fear of, and longing for, heroism is made poignant and understand-
able. One thinks of Hightower's soliloquy in *Light in August,* as he describes
the good bad boys of American literature. They are "boys riding the sheer,
tremendous tidal wave of desperate living. Boys. Because this. This is beautiful. Listen. Try to see it. Here is that fine shape of eternal youth and virginal desire which makes heroes. That makes the doings of heroes border so
close upon the unbelievable that it is no wonder that their doings must
emerge now and then like gunflashes in the smoke, and that their very
physical passing becomes rumor with a thousand faces before breath is out
of them, lest paradoxical truth outrage itself."[19] Hannah's fiction often exhibits the style of this passage, which is, for Faulkner, unusually terse. But
where Faulkner's prose here is straightforward, solemn, and even elegiac,
Hannah's is ironic, if nostalgic, in *Never Die.* The irony is also spiced with
the ludicrous, not only in Doc Fingo's inordinate pride at having "once
mended a broken dog" but also in the laughable military metaphors of his

19. Faulkner, *Light in August,* 458.

"leading an assault on his own shame" while he cowers in his office, and of the beating of his pulse as a sort of "cavalry in his ears, his own craven blood pouting away" (137).

In other stories, however, Hannah's narrative directly evokes the excitement of a boy in a grownup danger that is expressed both by Fingo and by Faulkner's Hightower. For example, when on a hunting trip with his father in "Uncle High Lonesome," young Pete finds himself, like Fingo, "in the manly world of men and armed conflict" (*ND,* 137). As the boy tells it,

> My father had put me down in a place they were hunting toward. Their guns were coming my way. Between me and them I knew there were several coveys of quail to ground, frozen in front of the dogs. . . . I was not much concerned. . . . In fact I was excited to be receiving fire, real gunfire, behind my tree . . . [and] now I would be a veteran. Nobody could touch me at war. . . . I was happy to see them approach this way, champion enemy cavalry, gun barrels toward me, a vantage not many children in their protected childhoods would be privileged to have. . . . The shot ripped through all the leaves around. This I adored. (*HL,* 213–15)

Much of the felicity of Hannah's language-based humor is related to the hyperbole that results from inappropriately juxtaposed parts of speech, a method that Mark Twain is so justly famous for. One thinks, for example, of *Life on the Mississippi* and young Sam Clemens, the narrating cub pilot, who says of the mate of the Paul Jones that "in the matter of profanity he was sublime." In a similar vein in *Never Die,* Kyle Nitburg, who has made himself judge and owner of the town, is "exquisitely friendless" (30).[20]

The title of *Never Die* is an intertextual clue that looks toward two major cultural mythologies that underlie much of Hannah's fiction: those of war and of the Old West, a connection Hannah himself has made in his comment to R. Vanarsdall about the J. E. B. Stuart stories: that "Stuart has a western flavor." The principal allusion in the title of *Never Die* is, of course, to General MacArthur's famous statement, "Old soldiers never die, they just fade away"; but it also suggests the undying myth of the Old West.

---

20. Samuel L. Clemens [Mark Twain], *Life on the Mississippi* [1883], ed. J. C. Levenson (Minneapolis, 1967), 38.

Hannah's tribute to the myth in this novel is part of a long American love affair with the West and with westerns, as the continuing popularity of Louis L'Amour's fiction attests (and perhaps the title of *High Lonesome* is his tribute to L'Amour, whose novel of the same name was published in 1962). Hannah's nostalgic western parody, *Never Die,* is every bit as romantic in spirit as are the L'Amour novels. Nevertheless, even a cursory glance at the dust jacket for *Never Die* suggests the postmodern nature of Hannah's book: the title, composed of block letters the color of golden sand, seems to deconstruct itself before the reader's eyes. The first word, "NEVER," like the familiar giant "HOLLYWOOD" sign on a California hillside, stands diagonally, in a bright light, casting a long slanting shadow on a gravelly textured red-orange background and also partly over the word "DIE," which is lying down as if dead or dying. Yet even this "dying" part of the mythic coda continues to cast a shadow, as do the cultural and literary traditions relating to the Old West.[21]

The intertextuality of *Never Die* is so pervasive that it approaches the high camp of John Barth's attempts in *The Sot-Weed Factor* and *Lost in the Funhouse* to rejuvenate the exhausted possibilities of the novel, and of Vladimir Nabokov's postmodern classic *Pale Fire.* According to Barth, just as Nabokov's "facing mirrors . . . suggest dizzying multiples" of character, so does Hannah's allusive prose suggest that his characters are the doubles of many historical and literary personae. On the one hand, the Reverend McCorkindale in *Never Die* is an avatar of Nathaniel Hawthorne's gloomy Reverend Mr. Hooper in "The Minister's Black Veil," whose veil symbolizes "secret sin." Hannah's reverend wears "the long black coat and the immensely brimmed hat, as if to avoid the light he was sworn to deliver to his flock" (*ND,* 17). Even Hannah's allusions to the way his reverend breathes parody Hawthorne's description of Minister Hooper: "a subtle power was breathed into [Mr. Hooper's] words" when he wore the veil, and his congregation "longed for a breath of wind to blow aside the veil." Hannah's minister wears "a black robber's kerchief on him, preaching under it, sucking in and blowing out. You could see nothing much but his eyes, hot and suffer-

21. Vanarsdall, "The Spirits Will Win Through," 331; Louis L'Amour, *High Lonesome* (New York, 1962).

ing" (57). On the other hand, the veiled minister, a lonely masked man, is a type of shadowy Lone Ranger—one who projects "something of the night"—to the citizens of the frontier town in *Never Die.*[22]

That Hannah can be discussed in terms of Barth and Nabokov is one measure of the postmodernity of his fiction. For Hannah and many other contemporary writers, literature is neither the "mirror" that reflects nature nor the "lamp" that throws new light upon it, to use M. H. Abrams' terms. It is, rather, a fiction that speech-act theorists call "performance literature," that is, according to J. Hillis Miller, "a way of doing things with words . . . [that] makes something happen in the real world." Like the music of Hannah's protagonist in *Boomerang,* it "make[s] something happen in vacant air . . . [that is] a sweet revenge on reality" (17). What Hannah's narrative does with words, which is both through and beyond storytelling, is analogous to what Miller attributes to classics like *Oedipus Rex:* it gives narrative form to human confusions (tries to explain the ambiguous human animal), while it dramatizes the danger of telling by convicting the teller. And yet because it does give narrative form to the shapes of human discontinuity and self-transformation, it mirrors reality after all.[23]

A Hannah protagonist, who is essentially the same character reborn in each new work, is a contemporary creation of the antihero with traits of the "roarer" on the American frontier; the *schlemiel,* who laughs to keep from weeping; and *homo ludens,* in the gender-specific sense, man at play. As in the traditional *bildungsroman,* Hannah's adolescents seek to be transformed by adult male experiences, as the narrator of "Repulsed," from Hannah's most recent collection, *High Lonesome,* seeks the efficacy of "strong drink and large women" (153). But they receive more than physical initiation from these women; Hannah's protagonists are also "gnawed and thrashed by [the women's] awful stories" (154); indeed, in Hannah's fiction, all life is measured by, and measured out in, story. In "Repulsed," New York City is "where the dregs of all stories [are]" (155); the young pro-

---

22. John Barth, "The Literature of Exhaustion," in *Surfiction;* ed. Federman, 30; Nathaniel Hawthorne, "The Minister's Black Veil," in *Heath Anthology of American Literature,* ed. Lauter *et al.,* I, 2138–2146.

23. M. H. Abrams, *The Mirror and the Lamp: Romantic Theory and the Critical Tradition* (New York, 1953), 57–59; J. Hillis Miller, "Narrative," in *Critical Terms for Literary Study,* ed. Frank Lentricchia and Thomas McLaughlin (Chicago, 1990), 69, 72–74.

tagonist has been "for years a mere roving hole of audiation, a great ear," listening to others' stories before he "finally [gets his] story out . . . [with its] terrible design" (155). The high-school student has traveled to New York City for a national band contest, where he has had his trumpet stolen by "a bum with perfect pitch" who had heard him play (155). More than an initiation story, "Repulsed" is also a commentary on the homeless poor, with one of whom the adolescent identifies because the beggar's face is scarred with acne, which the narrator sees as a mark of his "old teenagehood" (157). When the boy thinks, "Maybe he was me in my old age," it is clear that the two are another of Hannah's pairs of alter egos (158). The identification is more complex, however, and it develops throughout the story, as both characters are seen to be outcasts—beggars, repulsed by and repulsive to others, and vehicles for unarticulated stories.

Like many of Hannah's stories, "Repulsed" has a strong religious subtext and employs a wide range of biblical language, suggesting a storyteller's dependence upon the ur-story in the Bible. The protagonist has sulked silently for the "millennia" since puberty; he "pray[s] to be firm . . . even to be sullen in . . . adolescence"; he wants falling nuts from the orchard to "smite" him; even a leafless tree seems "in its March [Easter?] agony" (153); and he believes that his mother has "witnessed against" him (164). He is infatuated with an older woman next door, whom he watches through his window; and he relates a recurring surreal dream of her, "eating an enormous . . . loaf of . . . buttered French bread afloat there at her lips," as though it were a Daliesque vision of the Eucharist (154). He thinks she is "Mediterranean . . . or . . . a tropical Jewess" (155). He lives in a "town with a surplus of flanking churches where the unctuous and the grim were sanctified" (154); his parents want him to be like "the Good Steward" in the Bible (159); and eventually he decides to become a church trumpeter, because "many horns, hundreds, were in the Scriptures" (160). He also wonders if he is "becoming a little Christian," but that idea is immediately undermined by his seeming to equate belief with pretending: it was "nice," he confesses, 'to . . . believe in God . . . [and] to pretend I had girlfriends and deep acquaintances" (163).

One of the most important intertextual uses of the Bible in "Repulsed" is its extended metaphor of beggars and begging, which encompasses biblical stories of the Prodigal Son (Luke 15:1–32), the Good Samaritan (Luke

10:30–37), and the Paralytic at the Pool of Bethesda (John 5:2–9). Another is its title, which suggests the Fourth Song of the Suffering Servant,
seen as a prophecy of the Messiah, who was "despised and rejected by men;
a man of sorrows and acquainted with grief" (Isaiah 53:3). The theme con-
necting these stories to the adolescent's narrative is that of his love for the
older woman and especially for the homeless man. The boy is touched by
the old beggar's "persistence in the thin clothes under the tall optimistic hat
as the chill of the mongrel city went inward to your marrow, then grew like
a vine around your feet. I began to love the man," he confesses. "It started
in pity as I saw him huddle, then hunker, some special wind from Maine
smashing his pride. . . . All the iron in me fled as love took over." And the
story of his love is a "riff" described in musical terms, too: "Love is a buttered clarinet," the boy declares. "You've barely touched the instrument but
begin your wretched toots on the alien thing" (157). At the end of the story,
we realize that it is being told from the narrator's old age and that although
his life has been "slow and mistimed . . . [and] melancholy," he has found
it "good," even joyful. He "dare[s] . . . disgusted counselors . . . to argue"
(166); thus his joy is consonant with that depicted in the Gospel, wherein
a comic plot—that of the salvation of the world—depends on a scapegoat
who bears others' transgressions for the purpose of their regeneration: their
overcoming of the world.

Hannah's reliance, through biblical allusions, on not only the techniques but also on the attitude of the ancient comic tradition of the carnivalesque, identifies his work with the romantic revolution in literature that
Erich Auerbach sees as being directly related to the story of Jesus' crucifixion and resurrection:

> The revolution early in the nineteenth century against the classical doctrine
> of levels of style could not possibly have been the first of its kind. The barriers
> which the romanticists and the contemporary realists tore down had been
> erected only toward the end of the sixteenth century and during the seven-
> teenth by the advocates of a rigorous imitation of antique literature. Before
> that time, both during the Middle Ages and on through the Renaissance, a
> serious realism had existed. It had been possible in literature as well as in the
> visual arts to represent the most everyday phenomena of reality in a serious
> and significant context. The doctrine of the levels of style had no absolute va-

lidity. However different medieval and modern realism may be, they are at one in this basic attitude. And it had long been clear to me how this medieval conception of art had evolved, and when and how the first break with the classical theory had come about. It was the story of Christ, with its ruthless mixture of everyday reality and the highest and most sublime tragedy, which had conquered the classical rule of styles.[24]

Thus, Hannah's most significant connection with Romantic literature is through its correspondences with the Bible's great tragicomedy, with that story's "high lonesome" drama of martyrdom at Golgotha and its ultimate hopeful, happy ending.

Hannah's concept of the high lonesome experience is not that of a showdown in a desert mountain pass, as it is in Louis L'Amour's novel, but rather that of psychic or spiritual alienation. Hannah's *High Lonesome* depicts riffs on life played out in terms of characters who are like Uncle Peter of the title story, "unable to reroute the high lonesomes" that afflict them (222). These stories focus on various high lonesome places of the heart and various ways in which such crises can result either in a character's "diminished heart," as in "Two Gone Over" (181), or perhaps in the heart's expansion, as in the selfless love that the beggar excites in the young protagonist of "Repulsed." For many Hannah characters, the high lonesome feeling is the result of some memory that is too terrible to face and that makes the sufferer turn to drink. In "Uncle High Lonesome," Little Pete, the narrator, has fond memories of a hunting incident during which he was caught in the line of fire between hunters and a covey of quail. Although he is "excited to be receiving fire, real gunfire, behind [a] tree" (213), his Uncle Peter blames and humiliates the boy's father for having put him in harm's way. Now middle-aged, Little Pete, ponders the high lonesome that has apparently caused his uncle's tirade. Pete knows that Uncle Peter had in his youth killed a man over a poker game but been acquitted and that his consequent guilt had probably caused his lifelong alcoholism. He also knows that at about the same time as the hunting incident, his uncle had observed a young girl making a sexual slur directed at the adolescent Pete. "Could it be," he wonders, "as simple as that my uncle saw, in his nervous rage and unnatural mood, that girl

24. Erich Auerbach, *Mimesis: The Representation of Reality in Western Literature*, trans. Willard Trask (New York, 1957), 489–90.

calling me down the road to sin, and he exploded? That he saw my fate
coming to me in my teens, as his had when he killed the man?" (229–30).
In an abbreviated device reminiscent of John Steinbeck's *East of Eden,* a
modern repetition of the Abel and Cain saga through three generations, the
closure of "Uncle High Lonesome" reveals that the narrator has dreamed
that he has killed a man and escaped conviction and, further, that he is telling this story to his nephew, who says that he also has dreamed it.

The high lonesomes may lead to such a radical disjunction of personality that the narrator describes himself as split into several characters. For example, in "Taste Like a Sword" two alter egos open the story: "Why are you
alive? they ask me" (*HL,* 139). The narrator relates what is a surreal experience in which he thinks that one of the others "will rise up and become me,
absorb me, he is impatient for my space" (140). The content and structure
of this story cohere in a narrative that shows Hannah in his most postmodern mode, where the nature of reality itself is an issue, and characters con-
jure up alternate realities and identities. Here some characters have no
names, and some have names that allude to absurdist drama. "I could be
Fagmost," speculates the narrator, whose identity is always in question, "or
I could be Jimmy with Mr. Beckett in the alley" (146–47). Moreover, the
discourse is heavy with ontological questions, not only "Why are you
alive?" and "When are you going to get out of my way, out of everything's
way?" but also questions of the characters' gender and even of their species:
"They could be two starfishes on a stage. You're not even a decent hole, he
goes on. Why aren't you a woman?" (139–40). They do not ask epistemological questions about the world. Rather, as if in a parody of Shakespeare's
Miranda, they wonder what world they find themselves in "that has such
people [as themselves] in't!" (*The Tempest,* V.1.181–84).

In "A Creature in the Bay of St. Louis," the high lonesome experience is
that of a young boy who catches a big fish that gets away but not before
pulling the boy underwater, where he has a death-resurrection experience.
In subject matter and in the tone of danger and adolescent excitement, "A
Creature in the Bay of St. Louis" is much like other Hannah stories and
also like the traditional American boy books, but the narrative style and the
diction exhibit a powerful romantic lyricism in Hannah that is far different
from his early stories of adolescent initiation, as well as from the acerbic,
stylized wit of most of his recent work. The dreamlike style of this story

suggests nothing so much as that of Eudora Welty's "The Wide Net." Also reminiscent of "The Wide Net" are some details of plot and image in "A Creature in the Bay of St. Louis," especially in its evocation of a watery world with a legendary sea creature that is both frightening and exhilarating to the young protagonist at a time of great change in his life. In Hannah's story, it is a "twenty-pound brownish-black monster the size of a garbage can lid attached to his leg, thrashing and sucking with its awful mouth" (*HL*, 47). It is an experience he can share with no one, but will "return and return to it the rest of [his] life" (51). Here, then, is another memory in the making for a Hannah hero, one that will lie in wait, no doubt, and may trouble him in middle age.[25]

High Lonesome is a much smaller volume than the previous collection, *Bats Out of Hell;* but in each of these books, one story stands out from those exhibiting postmodern techniques. In the latter, it is "Evening of the Yarp," which resembles an Ozark folktale of the oral tradition more than any contemporary story structure; in the former, the anomaly is "A Creature in the Bay of St. Louis," the style of which is somewhere between that of Faulkner's most romantic initiation story, "The Bear," and Twain's darkly comic psychological realism. Clearly, Hannah continues to experiment with fiction that demands and delights an intelligent readership, including critical commentators who are up for a linguistic blitz.

25. Eudora Welty, "The Wide Net," in *The Collected Stories of Eudora Welty* (New York, 1980), 169–88.

BIBLIOGRAPHY

Abrams, M. H. *The Mirror and the Lamp: Romantic Theory and the Critical Tradition.* New York, 1953.

Anderson, Don. "Comic Modes in Modern American Fiction." *Southern Review* (University of Adelaide, Australia), VII (1974), 152–65.

Anderson, Sherwood. *Winesburg, Ohio.* 1919; rpr. New York, 1960.

Auerbach, Erich. *Mimesis: The Representation of Reality in Western Literature.* Translated by Willard Trask. New York, 1957.

Augustine, Saint. *Confessions.* Translated by R. S. Pine-Coffin. London, 1961.

Axthelm, Peter M. *The Modern Confessional Novel.* New Haven, 1967.

Bakhtin, Mikhail M. *The Dialogic Imagination.* Translated by Caryl Emerson and Michael Holquist. Austin, 1981.

————. *Rabelais and His World.* Translated by Helene Iswolsky. Bloomington, Ind., 1984.

Barnes, Djuna. *Nightwood.* 1936; rpr. New York, 1961.

Barthes, Roland. *Image, Music, Text.* Translated by Stephen Heath. New York, 1977.

Beatty, Jack. Review of *The Tennis Handsome* by Barry Hannah. *New Republic,* April 18, 1983, p. 39.

Beidler, Philip D. *American Literature and the Experience of Vietnam.* Athens, Ga., 1982.

Bergson, Henri. "Laughter." In *Comedy,* edited by Wylie Sypher. 1956; rpr. Baltimore, 1980.

Bibby, Michael. "'Where Is Vietnam?': Antiwar Poetry and the Canon," *College English*, LV (1993), 158–74.

Bly, Robert. *Iron John: A Book About Men*. Reading, Mass., 1990.

Blythe, Will. "Hannah and His Sentences." *Esquire* (March, 1993), 55.

Bradbury, Malcolm. "Closer to Chaos: American Fiction in the 1980s." *Times Literary Supplement*, May 22, 1991, pp. 17–18.

Brinkmeyer, Robert H., Jr. *The Art and Vision of Flannery O'Connor*. Baton Rouge, 1989.

————. "Beyond the Veranda: Trends in Contemporary Southern Literature." Paper delivered at Oklahoma Foundation for the Humanities symposium entitled "Southern Fried Culture: A New Recipe, A New South, A New Conversation," Tulsa, Okla., March 1, 1996.

————. "Finding One's History: Bobbie Ann Mason and Contemporary Southern Literature." *Southern Literary Journal*, XIX (1987), 22–33.

Brooks, Peter. *Reading for the Plot: Design and Intention in Narrative*. New York, 1984.

Brown, Roger William. *Social Psychology*. New York, 1965.

Broyles, William, Jr. *Brothers in Arms*. New York, 1986.

Burke, James Lee. *In The Electric Mist with Confederate Dead*. New York, 1993.

Butler, Robert Olen. *The Alleys of Eden*. New York, 1981.

Cady, Edwin H. *The Road to Realism: The Early Years, 1837–1885, of William Dean Howells*. Syracuse, 1956.

Caputo, Philip. *Indian Country*. New York, 1987.

————. *A Rumor of War*. New York, 1977.

Cawelti, Scott. "An Interview with Barry Hannah." *Short Story*, n.s., III (1995), 105–16.

Charney, Mark. *Barry Hannah*. New York, 1991.

Chase, Richard. *The American Novel and Its Tradition*. Garden City, N.Y., 1957.

Clemens, Samuel L. [Mark Twain]. *Life on the Mississippi*. Edited by J. C. Levenson. Minneapolis, 1967.

Coleridge, Samuel Taylor. *Miscellaneous Criticism*. Edited by Thomas Middleton Raysor. 1931; rpr. Cambridge, Mass., 1936.

Cox, Joseph. "'Versifying in Earnest': Richard Wilbur's War and His Poetry." Paper presented at American Literature Association conference. Baltimore, May 24, 1997.

Crane, Stephen. "The Bride Comes to Yellow Sky." In *Heath Anthology of American Literature*. 2nd ed. Vol. II of 2 vols., edited by Paul Lauter *et al.* Lexington, Mass., 1994.

Faulkner, William. *Absalom, Absalom!* 1936; rpr. New York, 1951.

——. *As I Lay Dying.* 1930; rpr. New York, 1990.

——. *A Faulkner Miscellany.* Edited by James B. Meriwether. Jackson, Miss., 1973.

——. *Light in August.* 1932; rpr. New York, 1968.

Federman, Raymond, ed. *Surfiction: Fiction Now . . . and Tomorrow.* Chicago, 1975.

Fiedler, Leslie. *Love and Death in the American Novel.* Rev. ed., 1966; rpr. New York, 1992.

Ford, Richard. *Independence Day.* New York, 1995.

Forster, E. M. *Aspects of the Novel.* 1927; rpr. New York, 1954.

Franklin, Benjamin. *The Autobiography of Benjamin Franklin.* Philadelphia, 1964.

Gerzon, Mark. *A Choice of Heroes: The Changing Faces of American Manhood.* Boston, 1982.

Gilman, Owen W., Jr. *Vietnam and the Southern Imagination.* Jackson, Miss., 1992.

Goffman, Erving. *Stigma: Notes on the Management of Spoiled Identity.* Englewood Cliffs, N.J., 1963.

Gordon, Mary. *Good Boys and Dead Girls.* New York, 1991.

Gretlund, Jan Nordby. "Barry Hannah." *Contemporary Authors.* Vol. CX of 139 vols. to date, edited by Hal May. Detroit, 1984. 231–36.

Hannah, Barry. *Airships.* New York, 1978.

——. "All the Old Harkening Faces at the Rail." *Fiction,* V (1978), 132–35.

——. *Bats Out of Hell.* Boston, 1993.

——. *Black Butterfly.* Winston-Salem, N. C., 1982.

——. *Boomerang.* Boston, 1989.

——. *Captain Maximus.* New York, 1985.

——. "The Crowd Punk Season Drew." *Intro,* I (1968).

——. "Fire over the Town." *Southern Living* (October, 1982), 138.

——. *Geronimo Rex.* New York, 1972.

——. "Get Some Young." *Reckon: The Magazine of Southern Culture,* I (1995), 128+.

——. *Hey Jack!* New York, 1987.

——. *High Lonesome.* New York, 1996.

——. "Iron Pony in the Ozarks." *Condé Nast Traveler* (April, 1992), 162–67+.

——. "Midnight and I'm Not Famous Yet." *Esquire* (July, 1975), 58–60+.

——. *Never Die.* Boston, 1991.

——. *Nightwatchmen.* New York, 1973.

————. *Ray.* New York, 1980.

————. "Return to Return: Base Line to Net and the Dead Run Back." *Esquire* (October, 1975), 160–65.

————. "Ride, Fly, Penetrate, Loiter." *Georgia Review,* XXXVII (1983), 33–38.

————. "Rocket Launchers, Lust, Croquet, and the Fall of the West." *Esquire* (January, 1992), 82–84+.

————. *The Tennis Handsome.* 1983; rpr. Baton Rouge, 1995.

————. "The Tyranny of the Visual." *Southern Review* (University of Adelaide, Australia), (1992), 753–69.

Hassan, Ihab. "Focus on Norman Mailer's *Why Are We in Vietnam?*" In *American Dreams, American Nightmares,* edited by David Madden. Carbondale, Ill., 1970.

Hawthorne, Nathaniel. "The Minister's Black Veil." In *Heath Anthology of American Literature.* 2nd ed. Vol. I of 2 vols., edited by Paul Lauter *et al.* Lexington, Mass., 1994.

Heinbach, Ellen B., and Gale G. Kohlhagen. *Guide to West Point and the Hudson Valley.* New York, 1990.

Hemingway, Ernest. *A Farewell to Arms.* 1929; rpr. New York, 1957.

Herr, Michael. *Dispatches.* 1977; rpr. New York, 1991.

Hobson, Fred. *The Southern Writer in the Postmodern World.* Athens, Ga., 1991.

Jacobson, Marcia. *Being a Boy Again: Autobiography and the American Boy Book.* Tuscaloosa, Ala., 1994.

Jones, John Griffin. "Barry Hannah." In *Mississippi Writers Talking,* edited by John Griffin Jones. Jackson, Miss., 1982.

"Joyce Carol Oates: Writing as a Natural Reaction." *Time,* October 10, 1969, p. 108.

Joyce, James. *Dubliners.* 1914; rpr. New York, 1984.

Ketchin, Susan. *The Christ-Haunted Landscape: Faith and Doubt in Southern Fiction.* Jackson, Miss., 1994.

Kreyling, Michael. *Figures of the Hero in Southern Narrative.* Baton Rouge, 1987.

L'Amour, Louis. *High Lonesome.* New York, 1962.

Lohafer, Susan, and Jo Ellyn Clarey, eds. *Short Story Theory at a Crossroads.* Baton Rouge, 1989.

McCaffery, Larry, and Sinda Gregory, eds. *Alive and Writing: Interviews with American Authors of the 1980s.* Urbana, Ill., 1987.

McHale, Brian. *Postmodernist Fiction.* London, 1987.

Madden, David. "Barry Hannah's *Geronimo Rex* in Retrospect." *Southern Review,* XIX (1983), 309–16.

————. *Revising Fiction: A Handbook for Writers.* New York, 1988.

Mailer, Norman. *Armies of the Night: History as a Novel, The Novel as History.* 1968; rpr. New York, 1994.

Malone, Michael. "Everything That Rises." Review of *Airships,* by Barry Hannah. *Nation,* June 10, 1978, pp. 705–708.

Marowski, Daniel. "Barry Hannah." In *Contemporary Literary Criticism.* Vol. XXXVIII of 85 vols., edited by Daniel Marowski. Detroit, 1986.

Mason, Bobbie Ann. *In Country.* New York, 1985.

————. *"Shiloh" and Other Stories.* New York, 1982.

Merton, Thomas. *The Seven Storey Mountain.* New York, 1962.

Miller, J. Hillis. "Narrative." In *Critical Terms for Literary Study,* edited by Frank Lentricchia and Thomas McLaughlin. Chicago, 1990.

Noble, Donald R. " 'Tragic and Meaningful to an Insane Degree': Barry Hannah." *Southern Literary Journal,* XV (1982), 37–44.

Oates, Joyce Carol. *The Edge of Impossibility: Tragic Forms in Literature.* New York, 1972.

————. *Them.* Greenwich, Conn., 1969.

O'Brien, Tim. *Going after Cacciato.* New York, 1978.

————. *The Things They Carried.* Boston, 1990.

Olney, James. *Metaphors of Self: The Meaning of Autobiography.* Princeton, 1972.

Olsen, Lance. *Circus of the Mind in Motion: Postmodernism and the Comic Vision.* Detroit, 1990.

Percy, Walker. *Lancelot.* 1977; rpr. New York, 1980.

————. *The Moviegoer.* 1961; rpr. New York, 1989.

Phillips, Jayne Anne. *Machine Dreams.* New York, 1984.

Pleck, Joseph H. *The Myth of Masculinity.* Cambridge, Mass., 1981.

Pratt, Mary Louise. "The Short Story: The Long and the Short of It." *Poetics,* X (1981), 175–94.

Rafferty, Terrence. "Gunsmoke and Voodoo." *Nation,* June 1, 1985, pp. 677–79.

Ravenel, Shannon, ed. *Best of the South: From Ten Years of "New Stories from the South,"* selected by Anne Tyler. Chapel Hill, 1996.

Rourke, Constance. *American Humor.* New York, 1931.

Rousseau, Jean-Jacques. *Confessions.* 1781–88; rpr. Paris, 1959.

Rubin, Louis D., Jr. *The Mockingbird in the Gum Tree: A Literary Gallimaufry.* Baton Rouge, 1991.

Salinger, J. D. *The Catcher in the Rye.* 1951; rpr. New York, 1979.

Seib, Kenneth. " 'Sabers, Gentlemen, Sabers': The J. E. B. Stuart Stories of Barry Hannah." *Mississippi Quarterly,* XLV (1991–92), 41–52.

Shepherd, Allen. "The Latest Whiz-Bang: Barry Hannah's *Captain Maximus.*" *Notes on Mississippi Writers,* XIX (1987), 29–33.

———. "Outrage and Speculation: Barry Hannah's *Airships.*" *Notes on Mississippi Writers,* XIV (1982), 63–72.

———. " 'Something Wonderful to Tell': Barry Hannah's *Boomerang.*" *Southern Review,* XIX (1983), 75–80.

Simpson, Lewis P. Introduction to Part I of *The History of Southern Literature,* edited by Louis D. Rubin, Jr., *et al.* Baton Rouge, 1985.

Skow, John. Review of *Geronimo Rex,* by Barry Hannah. Washington *Post,* April 19, 1972.

Slotkin, Richard. *Regeneration Through Violence: The Mythology of the American Frontier, 1600–1860.* Middletown, Conn., 1973.

Smith, Lillian. *Killers of the Dream.* Rev. ed., 1961; rpr. New York, 1994.

Spikes, Michael P. "Barry Hannah in the American Grain." *Notes on Mississippi Writers,* XXIII (1991), 30.

———. "What's in a Name?": A Reading of Barry Hannah's *Ray.*" *Mississippi Quarterly,* XLII (1988–89), 69–82.

Sukenick, Ronald. *In Form: Digressions on the Art of Fiction.* Carbondale, Ill., 1985.

Todorov, Tzvetan. *The Poetics of Prose.* Translated by Richard Howard. Ithaca, 1977.

Tregaskis, Sharon. "Pynchon's Cool." *Cornell Magazine* (September, 1996), 104.

Twain, Mark. [Samuel Langhorne Clemens]. *Adventures of Huckleberry Finn.* Edited by Sculley Bradley, Richmond Croom Beatty, and E. Hudson Long. New York, 1962.

Updike, John. "From Dyna Domes to Turkey-Pressing." Review of *Geronimo Rex,* by Barry Hannah. *New Yorker,* September 9, 1972, pp. 121–24.

Vanarsdall, R. "The Spirits Will Win Through: An Interview with Barry Hannah." *Southern Review,* XIX (1983), 317–41.

Vitale, Tom. Interview with Barry Hannah. In *A Moveable Feast.* Radio Series Broadcast #9403. 1993; rpr. on audiotape as *Barry Hannah Reads Stories from His Collection "Bats Out of Hell."* Columbia, Mo., 1993.

Waller, Gary F. *Dreaming America: Obsession and Transcendence in the Fiction of Joyce Carol Oates.* Baton Rouge, 1979.

Watson, James Gray. "William Faulkner: Self Presentation and Performance." Paper presented at South Central Modern Language Association conference, San Antonio, October, 1996.

Welty, Eudora. *The Collected Stories of Eudora Welty.* New York, 1980.

———. *The Eye of the Story.* New York, 1978.

Woodward, C. Vann. *The Burden of Southern History.* Rev. ed. Baton Rouge, 1968.

Wolfe, Thomas. *Of Time and the River.* 1935; rpr. New York, 1944.

Woolfolk, Robert L., and Frank C. Richardson. *Sanity, Stress, and Survival.* New York, 1978.

Wyatt, David. *Out of the Sixties: Storytelling and the Vietnam Generation.* New York, 1993.

Wyatt-Brown, Bertram. *Honor and Violence in the Old South.* New York, 1986.

Index

Abrams, M. H., 126

Absurd: literature of the, 4, 106; theater of the, 130

Aldrich, Thomas Bailey, 12

American Adam, 65, 91, 94

American colonies, 105

American Dream, 3, 10–11, 20, 21–22, 26, 40, 65

Ancient Mariner, figure of, 31, 38, 67. *See also* Coleridge, Samuel T.

Anderson, Don, 117–18, 120*n*16

Anderson, Sherwood, 4, 11, 73–74

Auerbach, Erich, 89, 128

Augustine, Saint, 31–32, 37

Axthelm, Peter M., 31–32, 37

Bakhtin, Mikhail M.: 67; *Rabelais and His World,* 73, 117–18

Baldwin, James, 5, 115

Barnes, Djuna: *Nightwood,* 121

Barrie, J. M., 61. See also *Peter Pan*

Barth, John, 68, 120, 125–26

Barthelme, Donald, 120

Barthes, Roland, 66

Beatty, Jack, 39*n*35

Beckett, Samuel: allusion to, in "Taste Like a Sword," 130; *Waiting for Godot,* 100

Beidler, Philip D., 43, 47, 54, 70–71

Bellow, Saul, 11, 31, 37, 70

Bergson, Henri, 105

Bibby, Michael, 50

Bible: 46, 130; language of, 2; as primary source for narrative, 104–105; as subtext in "Repulsed," 127–28

Bierce, Ambrose, 117

Bloom, Harold, 56, 104

Bly, Robert, 28–29, 31, 38

Blythe, Will, 114

Borges, Jorge Luis, 120

Bradbury, Malcolm, 69–70

Bradford, William, 11, 105

Brinkmeyer, Robert H., Jr., 1, 5, 21, 71

Brooks, Peter, 16, 32, 34

Brontë, Charlotte: *Jane Eyre,* 67

Brontë, Emily: *Wuthering Heights,* 100

Brown, Charles Brockden, 11, 71

Brown, Roger William, 39

Burke, James Lee: *In the Electric Mist with Confederate Dead,* 50–51

Butler, Robert Olen, 50

Byron, George Gordon, Lord: *Manfred,* figure of, 100

Cady, Edwin H., 17
Caputo, Philip, 44; *Indian Country,* 50
Carnivalesque, the: 5, 18, 73, 128; Bacchic atmosphere of, 119; Bible in comic tradition of, 128–29; literary techniques of, 118–19
Carver, Raymond, 70
Cawelti, Scott, 19, 114
Cervantes, Saavedra Miguel de, 106. See also *Don Quixote;* Don Quixote, figure of
Chappell, Fred, 5, 115, 116
Charney, Mark, 44, 68, 99
Chase, Richard, 94
Christ: as carnivalesque figure, 118; crucifixion of, as *scandale du monde,* 99; figure, 66, 68; -haunted South, 2; story of, as realistic tragedy, 129. *See also* Bible
Christian: as carnivalesque figure, 119; character in "Fans," 85; Hannah's upbringing as, 2; morals, 19; parodies of, 64–66, 81, 83; southern slaveholder as, 41; symbols in Hannah's fiction, 65, 81, 83, 127–28; vernacular, 2, 127
Civil rights movement. *See* Political movements
Civil War. *See* War
Clemens, Samuel Langhorne. *See* Twain, Mark
Coleridge, Samuel Taylor, 111–12. *See also* Ancient Mariner, figure of
Confederacy: 49; cause of, 25; characters representing, 52–55, 72, 89–90; painful memories associated with, 102; symbol of, 62, 96
Cooper, James Fenimore: 11, 71; as creator of the "American Adam," 94

Cox, Colonel Joseph, 36n31
Crane, Stephen: 11, 117; "The Bride Comes to Yellow Sky," 93–94, 120–22
Crews, Harry, 1
Cult of youth, 4, 61

Davis, Miles, 114
DeLillo, Don, 70
Derrida, Jacques, 16
Desert Storm. *See* War
De Soto, Hernando, 97
Dinesen, Isak: "The Cardinal's First Tale," 104
Donoghue, Denis, 66
Don Quixote, 106
Don Quixote, figure of, 78, 104, 118, 122
Dos Passos, John, 70
Dreiser, Theodore, 70
Dylan, Bob, 114

Eden: American, 67; dream of, 26; parody of, 64–65. *See also* American Dream
Edwards, Jonathan, 11
Eliot, T. S., 43, 79, 81, 112
Elitism, 117
Enlightenment, Age of, 10, 27
Existentialism, 2, 5, 19, 24, 33, 37, 39, 83

Farrell, James T., 70
Faulkner, William: 3, 7, 38, 45, 74, 102
—fiction of: *Absalom, Absalom!,* 25–26; *As I Lay Dying,* 96, 107–109; "Barn Burning," 26; "The Bear," 24, 131; *Light in August,* 117–18, 120, 123–24; *The Sound and the Fury,* 28, 108
Federman, Raymond, 68, 96
Feminism. *See* Political movements
Fiedler, Leslie: *Love and Death in the American Novel,* 10–11, 13, 120
Flaubert, Gustave: *Sentimental Education,* 8
Flynn, Errol, 81

Ford, Richard: 70; *Independence Day,* 93
Forster, E. M., 17
Franklin, Benjamin, 12
Freud, Sigmund: *Beyond the Pleasure Principle,* 16; *Jokes and Their Relation to the Unconscious,* 107
Frontier, American, 59, 120. *See also* West, American
Frost, Robert: "Mending Wall," 90

Game playing, 118–23. See also *Homo ludens*
Garland, Hamlin, 12
Gender: confusion, 63; cultural ideas about, 23, 40
Generation X, 82
Geronimo, 14
Gerzon, Mark, 27, 32
Gide, André, 6
Gilman, Owen W., Jr., 44, 96, 98
Gordon, Mary, 120
Gothic: grotesque, 33, 106, 107; neo-, 51; parody of, 33; southern, 3, 20–21, 118
Gregory, Sinda, 7n4, 19, 40
Gretlund, Jan Nordby, 14–15
Grimm's fairy tales: "Iron John," 29; "Hansel and Gretel," 94
Grotesque, 73–74. *See also* Gothic

Hannah, Barry: hometown and upbringing of, 2, 12, 47; as musician, 84; religious beliefs of, 14; as reviser of fiction, 59–60, 76–78, 109–10; substance abuse of, 81; as teacher of creative writing, 90
—books by: *Airships,* 3, 6, 20, 32, 38, 76–78, 86, 94, 109, 110, 115; *Bats Out of Hell,* 3, 6, 24, 47, 52, 59–60, 86–88, 91, 98–99, 114, 131; *Black Butterfly,* 81; *Boomerang,* 2, 6, 15–16, 24, 28, 30, 31, 37, 101, 107, 110–12, 126; *Captain Maximus,* 6, 24, 28, 39, 56, 68, 78, 82,

99, 109; *Geronimo Rex,* 1–2, 5, 17–19, 21, 23–24, 30–31, 109–10, 115, 116; *Hey Jack!,* 2, 6, 31, 34–37; *High Lonesome,* 4, 6, 61, 98, 114, 125–26, 129; *Never Die,* 5, 6, 94, 119–26, 129, 131; *Nightwatchmen,* 2, 5, 17–18, 74, 93; *Ray,* 6, 21, 31, 70, 94–99, 101, 110, 115; *The Tennis Handsome,* 4, 6, 76–78, 107–109
—nonfiction by: "Fire over the Town," 116n13; "Iron Pony in the Ozarks," 79n7
—stories by: "The Agony of T. Bandini," 119; "All the Old Harkening Faces at the Rail," 87; "Bats Out of Hell Division," 52–55, 89–90; "Coming Close to Donna," 32–34; "A Creature in the Bay of St. Louis," 130–31; "The Crowd Punk Season Drew," 109–10; "Dragged Fighting from His Tomb," 112; "Drummer Down," 119; "Even Greenland," 56, 80, 85–86; "Evening of the Yarp: A Report by Roonswent Dover," 90–92, 115, 131; "Fans," 83–85; "Get Some Young," 4, 61–68, 71; "Getting Ready," 82–83, 85; "Hey, Have You Got a Cig, the Time, the News, My Face?," 57–59, 88; "High-Water Railers," 86–88; "Idaho," 39, 83; "It Spoke of Exactly the Things," 80–81; "Love Too Long," 32, 109; "Midnight and I'm Not Famous Yet," 48–49, 51, 77; "Modern," 101; "Mother Rooney Unscrolls the Hurt," 113; "Nicodemus Bluff," 24–25; "Power and Light: An Idea for Film," 28; "Quo Vadis, Smut?," 74; "Repulsed," 126–28, 129; "Return to Return," 76–77; "Ride, Fly, Penetrate, Loiter," 78–80; "Rocket Launchers, Lust, Croquet, and the Fall of the West," 59; "Scandale d'Estime,"

47, 94, 99–101; "Snerd and Niggero,"
113; "The Spy of Loog Root," 89–93;
"Taste Like a Sword," 130; "Testimony
of Pilot," 23, 47–48, 54, 116; "That
Was Close, Ma," 59–61; "Two Gone
Over," 74, 113, 129; "Two Things,
Dimly, Were Going at Each Other,"
92–94; "Uncle High Lonesome," 124,
129–30; "Upstairs, Mona Bayed for
Dong," 56–57, 61, 102, 112; "Water Li-
ars," 22, 39, 86–88, 94
Harris, George Washington, 107
Hassan, Ihab, 20
Hawthorne, Nathaniel: 11, 71; image of
butterfly in, 81; "The Minister's Black
Veil," 125; "My Kinsman, Major Moli-
neux," 8, 65; "Young Goodman
Brown," 81
Hemingway, Ernest: 3, 7, 11, 49, 63–64,
74; "Big Two-Hearted River," 63; "A
Clean Well-Lighted Place," 6; *A Fare-
well to Arms*, 36–37; fish stories of, 83;
For Whom the Bell Tolls, allusion to, 64;
iceberg principle of, 39; as non-
combatant, 45
Hendrix, Jimi, 54, 114, 116
Heroes: 4, 83, 120; hero-mentor character,
27; as "interesting monsters," 68, 78,
85–86; parody of, 63–64, 76–78, 122–
24, 126; southern figural, 53
Heroism: 23, 32; in cultural myth, 27, 60
Herr, Michael, 36, 43
Hesse, Douglas, 69
Higgins, Dick, 75
History: southern, 4, 42, 44; and the
hyper-real, 69–70; military, 44; parody
of world, 110–11, 113
Hobson, Fred: *The Southern Writer in the
Postmodern World*, 74–75
Homo ludens, 106, 126
Honor: code of southern, 44, 46–47; cul-
tural concern with, 60–61, 123

Howells, William Dean, 12–14, 17
Hugo, Richard, 39, 83

Ionesco, Eugène, 21*n*14
Irony, romantic. *See* Coleridge, Samuel
Taylor

Jacobson, Marcia: *Being a Boy Again*, 12–
14, 16, 29
James, Henry: "The Figure in the Carpet," 6
Jesus, 32, 83. *See also* Christ
Jones, John Griffin, 21, 38, 115
Joplin, Janis, 54, 114
Joyce, James: "Araby," 101; epiphanic end-
ings of, 5; *Finnegans Wake*, 88; intertex-
tuality of, 4; *Ulysses*, 88; theory of, of
writer, 6, 91

Knight figure, 19, 77–78
Kosciusko, General Thaddeus, 55*n*15
Kreyling, Michael, 53

Lacan, Jacques, 16
L'Amour, Louis, 125, 129
Language: excesses of, 83; Hannah's talent
for, 88; influences on Hannah, 120;
play of, 68, 96; speech rhythms, 2
Lee, General Robert E., 48, 53, 101
Leitch, Thomas M., 5–8, 45, 63, 102
Literary canon, 117
Literature of memory, 42
Lodge, David, 75
Lohafer, Susan, 33
Lone Ranger, 122, 126
Longstreet, Augustus Baldwin, 107

MacArthur, General Douglas, 35, 124
McCaffery, Larry, 7*n*4, 19, 40
McCarthy, Cormac, 1, 5, 120
McCullers, Carson: *The Ballad of the Sad
Café*, 84
McHale, Brian, 75, 86

Madden, David, 1, 24, 109–10

Mailer, Norman, 20, 70, 112

Malone, Michael, 20, 102

Marowski, Daniel, 19

Mason, Bobbie Ann: *In Country,* 50, 70–71; "Shiloh," 57

Mather, Cotton, 71

May, Charles, 104

Melville, Herman: *Moby Dick,* 67

Merton, Thomas, 31–33, 37

Metafiction, 5, 7, 69–71. *See also* Surfiction

Miller, J. Hillis, 126

Mississippi: civil rights movement in, 45; Clinton, 12, 47, 116; flatboatmen of, 106; Jackson, 46; Vicksburg, 46, 59

Morrison, Jim, 54

Music: as frame of reference, 114–16; Hannah's tone as "confluence" of, 116; jazz, 115; literary images of, 4; musicians, 86, 115–16, 119; rock and roll, 82, 114–16

Myth: of angel/whore, 29; cultural, 3, 11, 22–23, 27–29, 38, 40, 42, 45, 51, 53, 65, 72, 87, 124; Greek, 65; of Old West, 124–25; structure of, in modernism, 66; timeless realm of, 62; of Vietnam, 70; of the warrior, 72. *See also* American Adam; American Dream

Nabokov, Vladimir: 68, 120, 125, 126; *Pale Fire,* 63, 90, 91, 126

National Book Award, 31

Noble, Donald R., 31, 109, 115

Oates, Joyce Carol, 16, 20–22, 37

O'Brien, Tim: 51; *Going after Cacciato,* 49–50, 109; *The Things They Carried,* 43

O'Connor, Flannery, 2, 3, 19–21

Oedipal complex, 3, 65, 68, 80

Oedipus Rex, 126

Olney, James, 20

Olsen, Lance, 66, 103

Ontology: in postmodernist texts, 75; shifting realities in, 86

Oral tradition, 4, 88, 90–91, 131

Pavel, Thomas, 86

Percy, Walker: 2, 93; *Lancelot,* 19; *The Moviegoer,* 19

Peter Pan: 61; parody of, 63

Phillips, Jayne Anne: *Machine Dreams,* 70, 96

Pleck, Joseph H., 27

Poe, Edgar Allan, 5–6, 99

Political movements: civil rights, 3, 42, 45; feminist, 1, 3, 22, 27, 29, 42; masculinist, 28–29

Post-traumatic stress disorder (PTSD), 50

Pratt, Mary Louise, 92

Prenshaw, Dick, 37, 116

Price, Reynolds, 104

Pynchon, Thomas, 82

Quest of the Holy Grail, The. See Knight figure

Quisenberry, John, 38, 47

Rabelais, François, 118–19

Rafferty, Terrence, 38–39

Ravenel, Shannon, 24

Rebel Rockets, 98, 114

Rebel yell, 98

Reid, Ian, 6, 67

Religion: Hannah's beliefs, 14; in Hannah's fiction, 31; and narrative, 104–105; in South, 2

Richardson, Frank C., 27

Rohrberger, Mary, 7

Rolling Stones, 54

Romantic sensibility, 99, 102, 129, 130–31

Roth, Philip, 70

Rourke, Constance, 105–106, 117

Rousseau, Jean-Jacques, 32

Rubin, Louis D., Jr., 25

Salinger, J. D.: 11; *The Catcher in the Rye,*
    14–15, 23, 100
Seib, Kenneth, 72
Shakespeare, William: 80; *Hamlet* figure,
    76; *King Lear,* 100; *The Tempest,* 130;
    Timon of Athens, 63, 90
Shelley, Mary: *Frankenstein,* 100
Shelley, Percy Bysshe: "Ode to the West
    Wind," 99
Shepherd, Allen, 22, 40, 107, 109
Short story, theory of, 5–8
Simpson, Lewis P., 107
Skow, John, 19
Slotkin, Richard, 44
Smith, Lillian: *Killers of the Dream,* 41
Speech acts, 126
Spikes, Michael P., 56, 70, 97
Steinbeck, John: *East of Eden,* 130; *The
    Grapes of Wrath,* 65
Sterne, Laurence A.: 6, 103; *Tristram
    Shandy,* 88, 102
Storytelling: as primal need, 104–105; as
    theme in Hannah's fiction, 85–86, 88–
    90; by war veterans, 36–37
Stuart, J. E. B., 48, 53, 72, 84, 124
Sukenick, Ronald, 68, 97
Surfiction, 68, 96, 102. *See also* Metafiction

Tarkington, Booth, 12, 16
Tate, Allen: "Ode to the Confederate
    Dead," 46
Thomas, Dylan, 66
Tiresias, 66
Todorov, Tzvetan, 77
Twain, Mark: 11–13, 29, 107; *Adventures
    of Huckleberry Finn,* 13, 120, 124, 131;
    Life on the Mississippi, 124

Updike, John: 11, 23–24, 31, 70; "Rabbit"
    characters of, 101

Vanarsdall, R., 39, 116, 124
Van Halen, Eddie, 114

Vietnam: Americans in, 3, 50, 54; com-
    pared to Civil War, 44, 51, 71; com-
    pared to Louisiana swamp, 51;
    generation, 3, 42–43; literature of, 3,
    42–45, 50–51, 54, 70–71; and *The Ten-
    nis Handsome,* 77; protests against, 112.
    See also War
Vitale, Tom, 74, 88, 115

Waller, Gary, 16
Walton, Izaak, 82
War: 24, 29, 39; American Revolution, 11,
    27, 55*n*15, 59; Civil, 3, 14, 36, 38, 42,
    44–46, 51–55, 59, 71, 84, 89–90, 97–
    98, 101–102; of 1812, p. 105; heroic
    rhetoric of, 55; Korean, 35, 59, 61, 64;
    literature of, 3, 48, 49, 70–71, 89; mas-
    culine world of, 96; as metaphor for vio-
    lence, 43; Mexican, 54; Persian Gulf
    (Desert Storm), 3, 56, 59–60; Vietnam,
    3, 36, 38, 42–45, 47–51, 54, 58, 70–
    71, 95, 97–98, 112; World War I, 36;
    World War II, 18, 111
Warner, Charles Dudley, 12
Watson, James Gray, 28*n*23
Wayne, John, 27, 122
Welty, Eudora: 5, 7, 38, 92, 102; *The Opti-
    mist's Daughter,* 21; "Powerhouse," 115;
    "The Wide Net," 131
West, American: 5, 59; literature of the,
    120; myth of Old West, 124–25; paro-
    dies of, 93–94, 119–26
West Point, N.Y., 53, 55*n*15
White, T. H.: *The Once and Future King,* 90
Whitman, Walt: "Song of Myself," 91
Wilde, Oscar: *The Picture of Dorian Gray,*
    66
Wilderness, American, 65
Williams, William Carlos: "Spring and
    All," 90
Winthrop, John, 11
Wolfe, Thomas: *Of Time and the River,*
    100; *You Can't Go Home Again,* 70

Wolfe, Tom: *Bonfire of the Vanities,* 69
Wolff, Tobias, 70
Woodward, C. Vann, 42
Woolf, Virginia, 7
Woolfolk, Robert L., 27

Wright, Austin M., 7, 69
Writing: as frame of reference, 114; theme
   of, 88–92. *See also* Storytelling
Wyatt, David, 42–43
Wyatt-Brown, Bertram, 46